STRATEGY & TACTICS OF AIR WARFARE

Marshall Cavendish London & New York

Edited by **Will Fowler**

Published by
Marshall Cavendish Books Limited
58 Old Compton Street
London W1V 5PA

© Marshall Cavendish Limited 1979
This volume first published 1979

Printed in Great Britain

ISBN 0 85685 506 5

CONTENTS

AIR WARFARE

The first experiments

The Wright *Flyer* on its historic flight at Kill Devil Hills, Kitty Hawk. Its brief journey was the beginning of a new era in peace time travel and the prosecution of war.

On 17 December 1903, at Kill Devil Hills, four miles south of Kitty Hawk, North Carolina, the brothers Wilbur and Orville Wright, bicycle manufacturers from Dayton, Ohio, made what is generally regarded to have been the first manned flight in a heavier-than-air machine. Their aircraft, appropriately known as the *Flyer*, stayed in the air for about a minute on its longest flight before being overturned and destroyed by a strong gust of wind. With the possible exception of Otto Hahn's splitting of the atom in 1938, that flight in 1903 was the most important and far-reaching event of the twentieth century so far. It represented the realization of one of man's most persistent dreams, for he could now, like a bird, travel through air, free from the strictures of topography and, to a certain extent, from dependence upon the wind.

The Wright brothers were by no means the first to devote their lives to the dream, but were unusual in their belief that the answer lay in heavier-than-air contraptions. For centuries the ingenuity of man had been devoted to lighter-than-air machines, ranging from the Chinese man-lifting kites of 2300 years ago, to the successful experiments with hot-air balloons by Joseph and Etienne Montgolfier in the 1780s. But there were serious limits to such machines: all were dependent upon the wind – indeed, the majority were totally unusable in anything but the calmest conditions – and all lacked manoeuvrability, even in the hands of the most skilful pilot. As a result, although there were occasional bursts of military enthusiasm, with balloons being used for battlefield reconnaissance and observation, the art of flying was restricted to those who could afford it as a sport. Experimentation went on, initially along the lines of attaching oars or manually-operated airscrews to the balloons, and then, in the mid-nineteenth century by slinging a steam-driven engine beneath the gas-bag, but the problems remained. Man did not have the energy or muscle-power to direct a free-floating machine, and the existence of red-hot steam pipes next to a bag full of hydrogen or coal-gas was hardly the height of safety. Slight improvements were made at the beginning of the twentieth century, when the internal combustion engine seemed to offer possibilities. Indeed for a time the development of dirigible airships, notably by the German Count von Zeppelin, suggested a breakthrough, but overall the lighter-than-air machines were something of a dead-end. If speed and manoeuvrability were desired, very large engines had to be used and, as these were necessarily heavy, bigger

and bigger airships had to be built to get them off the ground. Eventually, they became so big that their aluminium or wooden "skeletons" could not bear the weight, leading to a number of spectacular accidents. All of which makes the Wright Brothers' achievement seem even more revolutionary.

It would be wrong to assume, however, that the 1903 flight was immediately recognized as an event of historic importance, or that a track to Dayton Ohio was beaten to congratulate the Wrights on their achievement. In fact, the international press barely covered the flight, and many of the reports that did appear were so inaccurate that foreign observers discounted their veracity. One of the few men who showed more than a passing interest was Lieutenant-Colonel J. E. Capper, Commandant of the Royal Engineer's Balloon School at Aldershot, but although he personally visited the Wrights and urged their invention upon the War Office in London for military purposes, neither the British nor any other government showed any real interest. Too little information was available and too many unrelated, yet potentially-fruitful experiments were going on elsewhere for the Wrights to receive the credit that was their due. Nevertheless, their achievement probably provided the impetus that was needed, for as early as 1909 viable aircraft, of widely-differing designs, had appeared in a number of countries, clearly based upon the experimental work of the two brothers. The dream of manned flight, in relatively fast and manoeuvrable machines, had finally become reality.

It is still less than seventy-five years – or slightly more than an average life-time – since that initial flight, and one only has to compare an aircraft such as Concorde with the original *Flyer* to realize how far and with what phenomenal speed the art of manned flight has developed.

However, man rarely uses his skills for purely peaceful means and, in common with so many other inventions, the aircraft was soon adapted to the purposes of war. Theoretically, the possibilities were limitless: by flying over the battle area, whether at sea or on land, the whole panorama of opposing forces could be seen at a glance, enabling more accurate intelligence to be gathered, more quickly; and the enemy could be attacked directly from the air (a possibility foreseen as early as 1670 by an Italian Jesuit priest, Francesco Lana). Nor did it take men long to appreciate the usefulness of carrying troops or supplies by air or, eventually, of destroying the enemy homeland

Above: Wilbur Wright at the controls of a later Model A in 1911. The pilot is now seated and the wing warping and rudder controls are separate.
Left: Orville Wright.

itself through aerial bombardment. The evolution of these practices and their effects upon both the strategy and tactics of modern warfare constitute the primary themes of this book.

Since both the strategic and tactical roles of air power as they have developed, basically from the First World War to the present day are discussed at length, an early definition of the terms "strategic" and "tactical" is necessary. In a war, if aircraft are used in direct support of armies or navies – hitting the *manifestations* of enemy armed power in the immediate vicinity of the battle area or contributing directly to the movement, supply or defence of land or sea forces – this is usually regarded as tactical, whatever the size or depth of the battle area.

If, on the other hand, they hit the *sources* of armed power in the enemy homeland, away from the battle area, with the aim of destroying or impairing the enemy's capability to produce such power, then it is regarded as strategic. Or to put it simply: the destruction of a tank or ship in the battle area is tactical, the destruction of the factory or shipyard which produced them, is strategic. The difference between the two is worth bearing in mind as a number of specific air-power roles are examined in turn – strategic bombing, reconnaissance and observation, tactical strike support and interdiction, airborne troop landings and air transport, naval support, and the maintenance of air space.

The possibilities of aircraft as potential weapons of war were first recognized in 1911. In the summer of that year the Italians, intent upon achieving a position of dominance in North Africa declared war on the Turks and occupied the town of Tripoli, then a Turkish possession. The Italian expeditionary force included a small air detachment under a Captain Piazza, which proceeded to demonstrate its usefulness not only in reconnaissance but also in elementary bombing, when modified hand-grenades were dropped on to a Turkish camp. Relatively little damage was done, but the feasibility of aerial bombardment, admittedly on a tactical level only, had been firmly established. The extension of this to a strategic level, with the bombs being dropped onto the enemy homeland and areas of war-production, followed almost as soon as the European powers entered their next major conflict.

In the First World War strategic bombing was begun by the Germans. The 1914 version of the Schlieffen Plan, designed to outflank and destroy the Western Allies before Russia could effectively enter the war in the East, included a project for the capture of Calais and its use as a base for aerial attacks upon southern England. The aims were unclear, although it may have been hoped that elements of the British expeditionary force, particularly its aircraft, would have to have been withdrawn from France to counter the threat, so making the German advance on Paris that much easier. In the event, however, the Germans did not get as far as Calais during the 1914 offensive, and the plan was dropped. Nevertheless, they did not give up the idea of aerial bombardment entirely, for in 1915 and 1916 Zeppelin airships – the massive end-products of the lighter-than-air experiments – regularly set out at night from their bases in northern Germany to harrass and attack the industrial towns of the north of England and Midlands. A few even managed to make the long and dangerous journey to London, which was always regarded as the prime objective, but little damage was done.

Even at this early date, however, a number of lessons about strategic bombing and its effects emerged. Despite the large size and slow speed of the airships, the first point to be noted was that defence against their incursions was apparently ineffective. The progress of the Zeppelins could often be tracked from the North Sea to their targets, but regardless of the number of interceptor fighters sent up against them, very few were shot down or even damaged during the early raids. This was partly due to the high altitude at which the airships, flew, for by the time the heavier-than-air machine had struggled up that far, the intruders had gone, and partly the result of poor defence co-ordination around the major English towns, which had not been expecting such attack. Even so, the advantage seemed to be firmly on the side of the offensive power. In addition, there were significant signs of panic among the civilian population whenever the Zeppelins were reported, regardless of the lack of damage incurred through their operation. Sir Basil Liddell Hart, the British armoured warfare theorist of the inter-war years, for example, witnessed a raid in late 1915, the effect of which, he stated, was such that "in the weeks that followed, thousands of the population streamed out into the surrounding countryside" whenever the sirens sounded, whether it was a false alarm or not. Gradually, the home-based fighter pilots learned to go up at night without causing more damage to themselves than the enemy, the numbers of anti-aircraft guns were increased around the major towns, and a number of Zeppelins were destroyed. But although the enemy virtually admitted defeat by late 1916, the lessons remained. They were to be re-inforced within the year.

In the spring of 1917 the Germans began a more serious strategic offensive, this time during the hours of daylight. They established air-bases in occupied Belgium and from these Gotha bombers began to attack England with immediate success. In one of the first raids on the south coast, ninety-five people were killed, and although a total of seventy-four interceptor fighters went up to attack the Germans, only one bomber was destroyed. This set the pattern for the future and, as the Gotha crews gained experience, London itself came under sustained attack. On 13 June 1917 twenty-one Gothas dropped bombs in the area of Liverpool Street Station in London, killing 162 people and injuring a further 432. A month later another raid killed sixty-five and injured 245. In both cases large numbers of fighters took to the skies, but with negligible results.

These raids were important as they determined the future of strategic air thinking, not only in Britain but also elsewhere. The casualty figures may seem small compared to those of the Second World War, when it was not unknown for over 100,000 people to be killed in one raid alone, but in the London of 1917 they caused public outcry, signs of panic and a significant diminution of war production as workers stayed at home

to avoid being caught by the bombers in crowded factories which were likely to be the primary targets. The Lloyd George Government reacted by setting up a special committee, chaired by the South African Jan Christian Smuts, to investigate the lamentable state of British air defence and recommend improvements. The Smuts Committee made two reports, the first of which dealt exclusively with the defence system over London and suggested an immediate increase in the numbers of anti-aircraft guns and fighter aircraft, even at the expense of the Western Front. This was privately regarded by the Committee members as little more than a sop to public opinion, and it was the second report, submitted in September 1917 (less than three months after the Gotha raids) that contained their true feelings and affected the development of strategic thinking.

Its central assumption was sweeping: "The day may not be far off when aerial operations, with their devastation of enemy lands and destruction of industrial and populace centres on a vast scale, may become the principal operations of war, to which the other forms of military and naval operations may become secondary and subordinate. . . ."

In other words, Smuts and his colleagues were of the opinion that in the bomber was to be found a potential war-winner, capable of destroying the industrial base upon which any technological nation's armed forces had to depend. Furthermore, they were obviously thinking that the German Gotha raids were merely the beginning of such an offensive against Britain, for they went on to recommend an immediate counter-offensive as the best, if not the only form of defence. For this reason it was proposed not only that the strength of British air services should be doubled, but that a large strategic bombing force should also be created. Since the formation and direction of such a force would lie entirely outside the experience of existing military or naval staffs, who controlled the Royal Flying Corps and Royal Naval Air Service respectively, it necessitated the institution of an independent Air Service, provided with a separate administration and general staff of its own. Opposition to this idea was strong, particularly among those who saw it as merely contributing to a weakening of the Royal Flying Corps on the Western Front, but a series of night-time Gotha and Zeppelin raids during the winter of 1917-18, which proved almost impossible to counter successfully, ensured the implementation of the Committee's reforms. On April 1 1918 the Royal

Air Force came into existence, owing its separate identity almost entirely to the concept of a strategic counter-offensive against German cities. Unfortunately, although an independent bombing force was set up in France, operating the new Handley-Page 1500 aircraft, the war was over before it could be really tested in action. A few raids were carried out, but for most of the time up to the Armistice on November 11 1918 the force operated in long-range tactical support of the Allied armies, hitting German fuel dumps, communications and reserves behind their front line.

There can be little doubt that this had a detrimental effect upon strategic air theory. The Smuts Committee had met and reported in considerable haste, confronted with a series of extremely successful air raids, and there is much to warrant a view that the evidence used by the Committee was unrepresentative of the true facts. If the German raids of 1917 are taken in isolation – something which Smuts was obviously obliged to do as they were the first of their kind – a number of conclusions appear to be valid. Firstly, that the bomber, with the element of surprise on its side, always holds the initiative and will more than likely be able to drop its load before interceptors can struggle up to its operating height. Secondly, that air defence is not a great deal of use, for exactly the same reason. Thirdly, that such attacks were to be the operations of the future, causing panic in the streets, widespread destruction of property and instant diminution of essential war production as workers are dehoused, demoralized and killed. Fourthly, that the only hope is for a counter offensive designed to do more damage to the enemy than he can ever inflict on you, resulting either in your victory or a nullification of the weapon through deterrence.

These were basically the conclusions of the Smuts

A Zeppelin L48 cruises majestically through the skies of the early 20th century — craft like her, and later the Gotha bombers, were to terrify Londoners with their day and night raids.

Committee and the reasons behind the founding of an independent Royal Air Force and it was indeed unfortunate that the First World War ended before they could be tested in a more general way. As it was, the strategic conclusions drawn from that conflict formed the basis upon which a number of air-power theorists built up the framework of an air strategy which, in general terms, continued to be believed and practised by many at least until the 1960s if not to the present day.

The most important and influential of these theorists was probably Guilio Douhet, an Italian who gained his air experience operating with the Allies against Austria during the First World War, although it is interesting to note that he was never involved in a strategic bombing campaign. As a theorist, he was certainly the most revolutionary of his time, for in his book *Command of the Air*, published in the 1920s, he took the lessons of the late conflict to their extreme. Two basic assumptions formed the framework of his theory: firstly, that aircraft were instruments of offense of incomparable potential, against which no effective defence could be foreseen; and secondly, that civilian morale would be shattered by bombardment of centres of population. Taking these ideas, he followed them through until convinced that, in the event of war, the side with the larger strategic bombing fleet would automatically gain complete command of the air, since no effective defence existed, and would end the war swiftly by bombing the civilian population into a state of panic which would force the enemy to sue for peace. As a natural extension, neither armies nor navies would really enter into consideration and would play merely subsidiary roles, mopping-up and occupying territory. It mattered little to Douhet whether the bombers flew by day or night, but it was to his mind essential that the air force enjoyed

complete independence of administration and command, for the simple reason that tactical roles in support of armies or navies were totally unnecessary.

Douhet was so sure of the correctness of his arguments that he even entered into rather spurious mathematical calculations and worked out exactly how many bombs would be needed to destroy a given area of a city. Basing his hypothesis upon the fact that one bomb from a Gotha in 1917 killed, say, five people and devastated twenty-five square yards of buildings, he simply multiplied these figures so that ten bombs would kill fifty people, one hundred bombs devastate 25,000 square yards of buildings. In retrospect, one can perhaps appreciate the false logic which this entailed – after all, bombs do not fall in an exact pattern twenty-five square yards apart – but Douhet seemed, at the time and in the absence of further evidence, to be so convincing that as late as 1939 the authorities were sure that in the first week of hostilities alone a city such as London would suffer up to 66,000 fatal casualties.

Hence the mass evacuation of children from urban areas and the provision of over 100,000 hospital beds in Greater London alone for potential air-raid victims in September 1939.

Douhet was not the only air theorist to think along these lines in the 1920s and 1930s. In America Brigadier William ("Billy") Mitchell, a serving airman, was so vociferous about the war-winning potential of aircraft and the lack of official interest in his ideas that he was eventually court-martialled and forced to resign his commission. He too was convinced that, in an age of aerial warfare, military and naval campaigns, particularly so far as America was concerned, were subsidiary to the main air effort, if not totally unnecessary. He pressed for the defence of the American mainland to be put into the hands of an independent air force, demonstrating his belief that the navy was obsolete in this sphere by destroying the ex-German battleship hulk *Ostfriesland* from the air in July 1921: a lesson for the future that was completely ignored. In addition Mitchell saw no reason why, in the event of war, America should not depend upon strategic bombing for, according to his theory, waves of self-defending bombers, gaining command of the air as they flew through it, would operate during the hours of daylight and hit vital parts of the enemy war machine, undermining his capacity to continue the conflict. Unlike Douhet, however, he saw no reason to terrorize the

Handley Page HP O/400

Engines *Two 350hp Rolls Royce Eagle VIII-cyl vee, water-cooled; four bladed wooden propellers.*
Crew *3, 4 or 5*
Span *upper wing, 100ft; lower wing, 70ft*
Length *62ft 10¼in*
Height *22ft*
Max speed *97.5mph at sea level*
Armament *nose, double .303in Lewis MGs on Scarff ring; dorsal, single .303in Lewis MG; ventral, single .303in Lewis MG, fired through fuselage chute*

Bomb load *16x112lb; 8x250lb; 3x520lb or 550lb; 1x1,650lb; a 'supply' of 25lb Cooper bombs*

1 *The Office: control-wheel and main dashboard of the HP O/400 pilot's cockpit. Lower left shows door to the forward cockpit.*
2 and **3** *The 1,650lb SN bomb, with the 25lb Cooper bomb displayed by personnel of 207 Squadron, 29 August 1918.*

10

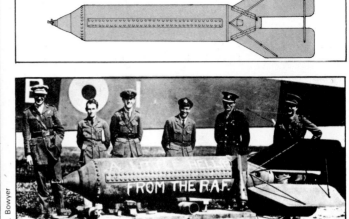

C. Bowyer

C. Bowyer

1 *Elevator*
2 *Upper tail-plane*
3 *Plywood tail cover*
4 *Aileron control horn*
5 *Steel cabane*
6 *Cabane braces*
7 *Port wings, shown in folded position*
8 *Fuselage frame*
9 *Dorsal .303in Lewis MG*
10 *Air-driven fuel pumps*
11 *Leading-edge gravity-feed fuel tanks*
12 *Forward entry hatch*
13 *360hp Rolls Royce Eagle VIII engines (2)*
14 *Radiator*
15 *Observer's seat*
16 *Pilot's seat*
17 *Twin .303in Lewis MGs*
18 *Access to gunner's position*
19 *Pitot tube*
20 *Pilot's foot controls*
21 *Slat flooring*
22 *Batteries*
23 *Fire extinguisher*
24 *Bomb bay below fuel tanks*
25 *Transparent panel*
26 *Faired rubber cord shock strut*
27 *Twin main-wheels*
28 *Fuel tanks (2) each holding 130 Imp. gall*
29 *Hinge strut*
30 *Plywood-covered spruce interplane struts*
31 *Plywood covering*
32 *Double flying braces*
33 *Drag strut*
34 *Aileron*
35 *Multi-strand cable bracing*
36 *Tailskid*
37 *Vertical stabiliser*
38 *Lower tailplane*
39 *Rudder*

civilian population, probably because he recognized that America could, with its huge industrial potential and lack of vulnerable land frontiers, maintain a bombing campaign for long periods, and did not, like Italy or other European powers, need civilian panic to end a war quickly. Despite his court-martial and failure to achieve an independent air force – the Americans continued to operate separate Naval, Marine and Army Air Forces until 1946 – some of Mitchell's ideas gradually took hold in America in the 1930s. The results will be examined later.

Meanwhile, what was happening in Britain, the source of so much evidence about strategic bombing and its effects? First of all, it needs to be made clear that neither Douhet nor Mitchell had a noticeable effect upon the Royal Air Force strategists. Despite a fairly widespread belief that Douhet's theories in particular affected the development of air power in all countries except Russia and Japan, it is highly improbable that many people in Britain between the wars had even heard of Douhet, let alone studied *Command of the Air*. It is probably safer to say that British air power, building on the considerable experience of the First World War, tended to develop on its own, expecially in the 1920s. There were two main reasons for this. Firstly, there was no need, immediately after the First World War, to pursue theories like those of Douhet or Mitchell, which had as their central theme the necessity for the creation of independent air forces, for the Royal Air Force had achieved its independence in 1918; secondly, as it had been formed specifically to carry out long-range strategic bombing, all the air administrators in London had to do to ensure a future strategic role was to maintain the *status quo*.

But this was not as easy as it sounds. Once the First World War was over, many politicians and military leaders pressed for the abolition of the Royal Air Force as an unnecessary peace-time luxury and the British air chiefs had to fight very hard indeed to maintain their independence. The fact that they succeeded was due almost entirely to one man – Hugh, Lord Trenchard. Born in 1873, he saw active service in South Africa, India and Nigeria as an officer in the Royal Scots Fusiliers before deciding, at the relatively late age of 39, that he wanted to fly. His regimental experience made him a welcome addition to the Royal Flying Corps – formed in 1912 as a unit of the Royal Engineers – when he transferred to it in the summer of that year. Between then and 1919 he progressed from Major to full General, holding nearly every important air post, including that of Commander of the Independent Bombing Force of the Royal Air Force in 1918, before becoming Chief of the Air Staff. He held the latter post from 1919 until December 1929 and was therefore in the forefront of the battle to maintain its independence. He succeeded in winning that battle by stressing three main points, and although it seems pertinent to describe him as an organizer and administrator rather than a theorist of air power, it is surprising how similar his final conclusions were to those of both Douhet and Mitchell.

Firstly, Trenchard was an ardent believer in air offensive, arguing that regardless of the numerical strength of the enemy, it was impossible to defend every cubic foot of air space above one's country. Just as it is extremely difficult to put up an effective barrier to a swarm of bees, some of which will simply fly round, above or below that barrier, so it was almost

impossible to prevent the passage of aircraft through all air space, at least in the context of the 1920s. For this reason, according to Trenchard, air defence was a waste of time and a negation of air power, since to devote aircraft and men to such operations would not prevent the enemy getting through in some form or other: you might inflict casualties but you would never stop him completely. Therefore, if the Royal Air Force was to be used, it had to be constantly on the offensive and, as his second point, because all Britain's potential enemies were situated a long way off, this had to be carried out by the long-range bomber. There was little room for co-operation in the tactical sphere with the Army or Navy, as this would merely dissipate valuable resources, and this in turn, as the final point, necessitated the continued independence of the Royal Air Force. It is interesting to note that Trenchard never said that his bombers would end the war without the need for military or naval campaigns, but he did feel that the strategic air offensive would be so vital to the overall war effort that no one could doubt its necessity.

As has been already intimated, Trenchard managed to persuade enough influential people round to his way of thinking to ensure that the Royal Air Force did not disappear, and when he resigned as Chief of the Air Staff in 1929 to make way for a younger man, it looked

as if the strategic bomber had been accepted in Britain as a potentially useful weapon for the future. Unfortunately, further efforts to undermine the autonomy of the R.A.F. were made in the 1930s – and it is in the light of the battles between military and naval administrators on the one hand and the air chiefs on the other, basically over who was to get what share of an increasingly stringent peace-time defence budget, that led Trenchard's successors to take his ideas one stage further, into the realms of the extreme. From his argument that air defence was not a great deal of use came the expression, first used by Prime Minister Stanley Baldwin in the House of Commons in 1932, that "the bomber will always get through" – something which Trenchard had never categorically stated. Similarly, in an effort to show that strategic bombing was not only viable but also essential, an argument which was designed to obtain an expansion of the Royal Air Force, the air chiefs began to expand their claims. Basing their opinions more and more upon the Smuts Committee and the effects of unopposed bombing by the Royal Air Force in places like Iraq and North-West India, it was argued that strategic bombers, operating by day, would be able to attack enemy cities with impunity, hitting selected targets of vital economic importance and rapidly undermining the morale of the civilian population. In the end, as it may be appreciated, the British ideas began to look very like those of Douhet and Mitchell, even though they were arrived at by different routes and for slightly different reasons.

At the beginning of the Second World War the various ideas, theories and specifically the aims of strategic bombing could be summarized as follows: the undermining of civilian morale, which would, it was hoped, force the enemy government to sue for peace; and the destruction of key targets which would destroy the capability of the enemy to wage technological war. The method of achieving one or both of these aims was to bomb by daylight and with accuracy, a method based firmly on the belief that the bomber would always get through.

What needs to be remembered before the validity of these ideas is examined in detail, is that in 1939 the theory of strategic bombing was just that, only a theory. It was based upon incomplete evidence from the First World War which had been taken to extremes by people intent upon achieving or maintaining air force independence, and had never been put into practice, so the problems and shortcomings were simply not known.

Strategic Bombing

The instrument of night strategic bombing — an RAF Lancaster taxis prior to take-off for a raid on Germany.

The three strategic bombing campaigns to be examined in this chapter are those against Germany and Japan during the Second World War and that against North Vietnam between 1965 and 1973. These are not the only campaigns which have taken place since 1939 – the German attacks on Britain in 1940 and 1941 are not included, for example, because they fit so conveniently into the Battle of Britain as a whole, which will be examined in a later chapter – but for the purposes of testing the validity of strategic theory they are by far the most important. In the course of this examination, the Allied attacks upon Germany between 1939 and 1945 will be emphasized, partly because they involved the air forces most affected by the pre-war theories and partly because they have been the subject of more research and comment than any other strategic attacks. This does not mean that less can be achieved by looking at Japan or North Vietnam as individual campaigns but it seems logical to use them to illustrate how poorly the lessons of the offensive against Germany were assimilated by those in high command. What those lessons were constitutes the central theme of this chapter.

When war broke out in September 1939 the bomber arm of the Royal Air Force was not prepared. It had a theory of strategic bombing worked out, based upon the two-fold assumption that the bomber would always get through and be able to destroy vital parts of the enemy's war-machine, but it had neither adequate equipment with which to carry this out nor experience upon which to base its course of action. In addition, the Chamberlain Government did not wish to initiate strategic bombing, not only because it might cause a reaction from the enemy that would be more devastating and decisive, but also because neutral countries whose aid might be essential in the future – notably America – would regard it as an unnecessary escalation of the conflict. After all, the Washington Conference on the Limitation of Armaments, held in 1922, had expressly condemned "aerial bombardment", and the American President in 1939, F. D. Roosevelt, was known to be opposed to unrestricted air warfare, even in a conflict which did not yet involve his country. Even before it had started, therefore, the theory of strategic bombing had come up against the problem of world opinion, which negated one of Douhet's basic ideas – that future wars would begin, and probably end, with waves of bombers devastating centres of civilian population. This problem was to appear again later.

Nevertheless, during the early "Phoney War" period of the Second World War, Royal Air Force Bomber Command did carry out two forms of limited attack upon the enemy homeland. Neither of these can be strictly termed as strategic in aim, but their existence was to have radical results upon future air policy. On the one hand bombers carried out daylight raids against enemy shipping, chiefly in the North Sea and the Baltic, and on the other they dropped leaflets over Germany itself by night. The anti-shipping raids, carried out by Vickers Wellingtons of No. 3 Group, failed to make much headway against German fighters and anti-aircraft defences and twice, in September and December 1939, the dispatched force lost 50 per cent of its aircraft; a loss-rate which if it had continued would have wiped out Bomber Command in less than a week. The British Air Staff began to realize that the heavy bomber could not survive in daylight, and this feeling was reinforced by the apparent success of the leaflet raids, for the Armstrong Whitworth Whitleys of No. 4 Group, operating at night, suffered few casualties. An idea arose – understandably enough – that a switch from day to night bombing might well be prudent. The basic aims of strategic bombing – the undermining of civilian morale and the precise destruction of key targets – were not to be abandoned, but the method of achieving them was to be revised. By May 1940 night bombing raids were becoming more frequent, and by the autumn of that year daylight attacks had virtually ceased.

Night bombing, however, created its own problems. During these early months of the offensive the standards of navigation and bomb-aiming were poor, and on most night-time raids it was lucky if the aircraft – designed for daylight operations and crewed by men who had been trained accordingly – actually reached the target, let alone hit exactly what they were aiming at. This was discussed as early as March 19 1940, before the switch to night bombing had even been ordered, when a group of fifty bombers attacked the German seaplane base at Hornum on the island of Sylt.

Most of the crews believed that they had located the target and placed their bombs accurately, but reconnaissance photographs the next day showed no sign of damage whatsoever. In fact at the end of the war it was discovered from captured German records that the enemy was completely unaware that any raid had taken place at all! This lack of effectiveness continued until August 1941 when Churchill's Scientific Adviser,

Lord Cherwell, was directed to organize an official investigation into the accuracy of the bomber offensive. His chosen investigator, a civil servant by the name of Butt, looked at some 600 aerial photographs taken by bombers after they had released their bombs on raids in June and July 1941.

Taking into account the necessarily selective nature of his statistics – after all, not every bomber had returned – Butt's overall conclusion was that of the bomber crews who thought they had located and hit a specific target, only about one third had managed to drop their loads within five miles of it. Thus the target area, far from being a circle of 300, 600 or even 1000 yards around an aiming point, as some optimists imagined and precision bombing required, was in fact a territory up to five miles in radius. Two bombs landing within this target area might be up to ten miles apart. Moreover, it was apparent that only a small proportion of the more successful raids were achieving even this degree of success.

The Butt Report showed the inevitable result of the switch from day to night bombing, and suggested that before the prospect of precision bombing by night could become a reality the efficiency and equipment of Bomber Command had to be much improved or an alternative mode of operations found. The obvious alternative was a return to day bombing, but since the "Circus" operations of summer 1941, this was regarded as still potentially dangerous. (When Germany invaded Russia in June 1941 the Russians insisted upon a bomber offensive in the West to draw German air power away from the Eastern Front, and the Royal Air Force obliged by mounting a series of daylight sorties, using both bombers and fighters over occupied France. At first with the protecting escort-fighters much in evidence, the Germans had refused to rise to the bait, but when the bombers came alone, the enemy fighters had a field day, which suggested that any return to daylight bombing as a central policy was sure to end in disaster.) In such circumstances, night-time raids had to stay but in the light of the problems of navigation and accuracy the method of carrying them out had to be revised.

The Chief of the Air Staff, Air Marshal Sir Charles Portal, produced such a revision in early 1942 when he suggested the substitution of area for precision bombing, so that in the case of a city or large town, the entire urban complex not merely the industrial targets within it, would be attacked. This had two distinct advantages, for on the one hand it would normalize the results already being achieved – if, as Butt said, the target area was being missed by five miles, then make the target area five miles square – and on the other it might achieve the aim of disrupting war-production not by hitting the factories but by de-housing, terrorizing and killing the working population. The new Bombing

17

Directive consequently appeared on February 14 1942 laying down specifically that the raids on places like Duisberg, Essen, Dusseldorf, Cologne and Berlin were now to be focussed upon the morale of the civil population and, in particular, its industrial workers. Precision attacks upon key targets were no longer to be the norm – although this did not preclude them entirely if the circumstances were right – and a note attached to the Directive by the Chief of the Air Staff emphasized the true nature of the new offensive, pointing out that in the urban attacks of the future "the aiming points are to be the built-up areas, *not*, for instance, the dockyards or aircraft factories." In other words, in a relatively short time, the original theory of strategic bombing as it had emerged by 1939, had been altered out of all recognition. Far from being an offensive of precision bombing by day, practical problems, unforeseen by the theorists, had turned it into one of area bombing by night.

Area bombing presented yet another disadvantage, however, for if it was intended to hit huge urban complexes night after night, as it had to be if industrial workers were to be demoralized to the extent that important factories no longer operated, a very large bomber fleet was needed – something which did not exist in early 1942. Furthermore, even if the aircraft were available, little was likely to be achieved unless it could be guaranteed that the majority would find the target in the dark and, once over it, drop their bombs in concentrations which would swamp the civil defence services and destroy large areas of urban housing and industrial facilities. In the light of these considerations, Bomber Command was in no position to carry out the Area Bombing Directive effectively in early 1942, and it is small wonder that it was around this time that pressure for an end to strategic bombing reached its height in Britain with influential politicians and military men pressing for a full-scale transfer of heavy bombers and their crews to tactical support or naval co-operation. If Bomber Command was to survive and strategic bombing to be tested to the full, a great deal of development had to take place quickly and a number of improvements made both to efficiency and equipment.

The first sign of improvement came on February 22 1942, only eight days after the Area Bombing Directive had been issued, when Air Marshal Sir Arthur Harris was appointed Commander-in-Chief of Bomber Command. He was wholeheartedly in favour of area bombing, later in the war he maintained what were known as

"Blue Books" showing, by means of perspex overlays on aerial photographs, the amount of damage done to German cities. He fully realized the need for a large bombing fleet, something which was unlikely to materialize in the prevailing climate of influential opposition. His first task, therefore, was to mobilize public opinion in his favour and gain official recognition for the bombing offensive, basically by making it appear more effective than it was. The method he and his Deputy, Air Marshal Sir Robert Saundby, chose was to attempt the seemingly impossible by organizing a raid to be carried out by 1000 aircraft. Nothing like this had ever been tried – indeed, in order to gather together 1000 planes capable of carrying bombs to Germany, Harris had to commit his entire front line force, its reserve and even elements of its training cadres – and the risks were frightening. Even at the accepted level of casualties (then about 5 per cent of any committed force), Bomber Command could expect to lose over fifty aircraft, and this took no account of midair collisions, aircraft being hit by falling bombs, or the dubious flying ability of some of the participating crews, particularly those who had not even finished their training. But the gamble paid off. When the British public was informed that on the night of May 30-31 1942 1046 bombers had attacked the city of Cologne, their approbation successfully vaporized official opposition. In the event, little irreparable damage was done to Cologne, but the relatively small losses sustained by the attacking force – forty-four aircraft, or 3.9 per cent – and the apparent strength of Bomber Command put the strategic offensive firmly back on the map. Any talk of transferring bombers to Coastal Command or tactical support in other theatres would now produce an immediate public outcry.

Having obtained this vital breathing-space, Harris set about improving the equipment and techniques of his command, bearing in mind throughout that he was involved in a night-time area campaign. On the equipment side he was fortunate improvements to air-

Left: Window tumbles through the sky. This was an early form of E.C.M. By dropping foil strips in the sky Allied aircraft could reproduce reflections on German radar that looked like incoming bombers. Below: A USAAF B-17 plunges down, disintegrating as it burns. American losses in daylight raids were heavy until they coordinated their fighter protection and flight patterns.

craft design had been taking place before he was appointed, for by early 1942 the twin-engined, short-range Wellingtons and Whitleys had been replaced by long-range bombers like the Short Stirling and Handley-Page Halifax. This development trend culminated in the introduction of the Avro Lancaster, the first few of which were ready for use in the Thousand Raid on Cologne. Developed from an abortive twin-engined machine known as the Manchester, the Lancaster was undoubtedly the best British bomber of the war. By 1942 the Stirling and to a lesser extent the

Halifax, had shown performance shortcomings, but the Lancaster seemed to offer a great deal of potential. Its four Rolls Royce engines were powerful, capable of carrying it to high altitude if necessary and fully able to lift large bomb loads. It was relatively fast, reasonably well armed for night flying and, most important of all, popular with the air crews.

But the development of such a good aircraft, although giving Bomber Command the means to do the job as early as 1942, was not a great deal of use as long as the problems of navigation and bomb-aiming remained.

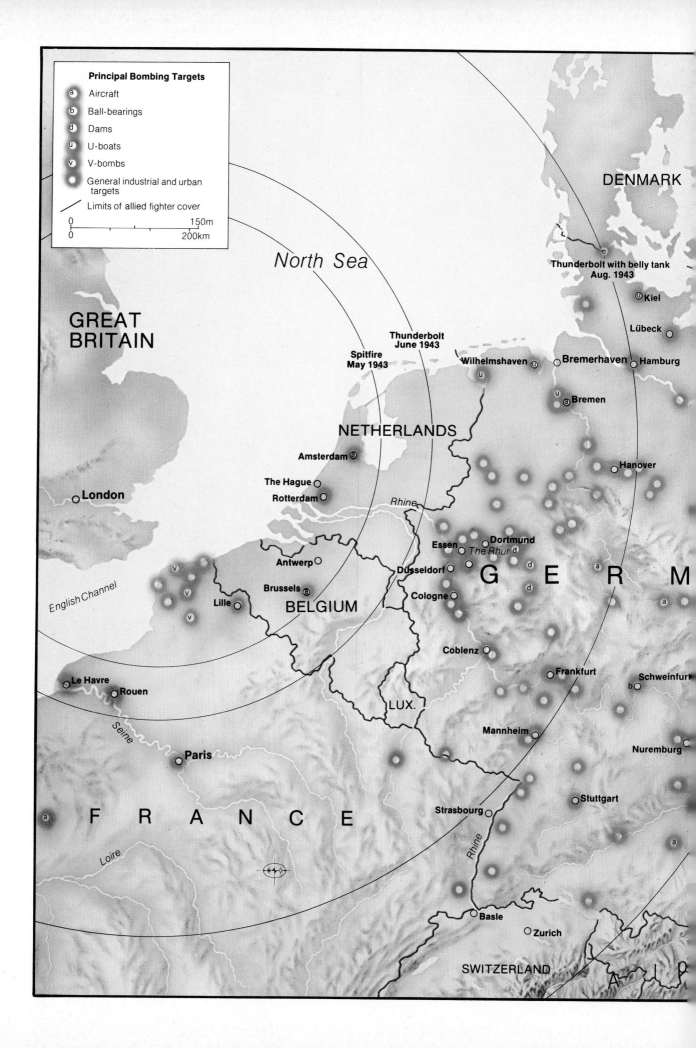

Principal Bombing Targets

- Ⓐ Aircraft
- Ⓑ Ball-bearings
- Ⓓ Dams
- Ⓤ U-boats
- Ⓥ V-bombs
- ⊙ General industrial and urban targets
- ╱ Limits of allied fighter cover

0 ——————— 150m
0 ——————— 200km

North Sea

DENMARK

Thunderbolt with belly tank
Aug. 1943

Ⓤ Kiel

Lübeck

**GREAT
BRITAIN**

Thunderbolt
June 1943

Spitfire
May 1943

Wilhelmshaven Ⓤ   ○ Bremerhaven   ○ Hamburg

Ⓤ
ⓤ

Ⓤ
Ⓐ Bremen

NETHERLANDS

Amsterdam Ⓐ

○ Hanover

The Hague ○
Rotterdam ○

Rhine

○ **London**

Antwerp ○

Dortmund
Essen *The Rhur* Ⓓ

G E R M

Düsseldorf ○   Ⓓ
Ⓐ

Brussels ○ Ⓐ

Cologne ○   Ⓓ

BELGIUM

Ⓥ
Ⓥ

Ⓥ Lille ○

Ⓥ

English Channel

Coblenz ○

Ⓐ

○ Frankfurt

Schweinfurt
Ⓑ

Le Havre ○
○ Rouen

LUX.

Mannheim ○

Nuremburg

Ⓐ

Seine

Ⓐ Paris

Stuttgart ○

F R A N C E

Strasbourg ○

Ⓐ

Loire

Rhine

Ⓐ

Basle ○

○ Zurich

SWITZERLAND

20

SWEDEN

Baltic Sea

Copenhagen

Mustang
Dec. 1943

Lightning
Nov. 1943

Peenemünde

Rostock

Stettin

Elbe

Oder

Berlin

POLAND

Magdeburg

a

N Y

Leipzig

Breslau

Dresden

Chemnitz

Prague

CZECHOSLOVAKIA

a

Danube

Vienna

a

Munich

Salzburg

AUSTRIA

The strategic bombing offensive against Germany by the RAF and USAAF hit civilian and industrial targets. The RAF had developed night bombing tactics principally because they did not have the protective firepower and fighter cover in the early years of the war. The USAAF took over day bombing, attacking industrial targets in an attempt to destroy Germany's munitions factories.

Fortunately, research had been carried out by air scientists and, even before the Area Bombing Directive had appeared, the first steps had been taken to improve these crucial aspects of the campaign. So far as navigation was concerned, a range of radar inventions helped the bombers to find the targets in the dark. The first of these, known as *Gee*, was available from early 1942, enabling a bomber's navigator to fix his position by consulting an instrument which received special signals from three widely separated stations in England. The instrument worked out the difference between receipt of these signals and gave an instant "fix", but did suffer from defects of range, being unable to operate more than 400 miles from the English coast because of the curvature of the Earth. In December 1942 a new device – *Oboe* – appeared, which enabled aircarft to follow radar beams to pre-selected targets, but once again effective range was restricted. It was not until January 1943, when a third invention – *H2S* – was introduced, that the navigator could be provided with a radar map of the ground over which he was flying and although this too had deficiencies, being most effective only when a contrast between land and water could be made, it did ensure a chance of arriving on target.

At about the same time it became common policy for the bombers to attack in a stream rather than individually or by squadrons. This was introduced initially to defeat the German defensive system known as the Kammhuber Line – a series of radar posts, anti-aircraft sites and night fighter stations stretching from Denmark to Northern France – which, by dividing the defended area into a series of "boxes" and stationing night-fighters in each, had managed to destroy many individual bombers. In 1942 the British realized that one way to defeat this system was to concentrate the bombers and swamp selected boxes, at the same time confusing German radar by dropping massive amounts of *Window* – small metal strips, cut to the correct wave length, which showed up on the radar screens as bomber formations and caused the enemy to commit his defending fighters away from the main attack. The scheme was an instant success. It even produced an unforeseen navigational bonus, for so long as the leaders of a stream found the target, all the other bombers had to do was follow the aircraft in front. As the leaders then tended to be chosen from among the more experienced crews (they being the most likely to locate the target correctly), it did not take long for their duties to be extended to include marking the target area, so that the

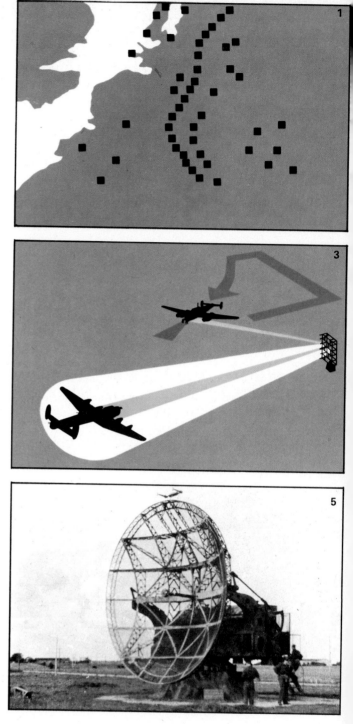

following waves had something definite to aim at and concentration of destructive power could be achieved. The effectiveness of this "Pathfinder" technique was shown as early as March 28 1942 when a selected group of bombers, operating the new *Gee* radar, was directed to mark the Baltic city of Lubeck with red flares and incendiaries. The results were impressive, with re- connaissance photographs later showing nearly half the city in ruins. Thereafter the idea was used on a regular basis. Indeed, by 1944, the stream leaders were not only marking the aiming-point but remaining over the target area to guide the other bombers in, which was usually the responsibility of a Master Bomber. When techniques like this had been fully developed, Bomber Command was potentially at its most effective.

Meanwhile, America had come into the war, and its vast human and industrial might promised a reinforce- ment to Bomber Command which should have made the campaign decisive. But this did not happen immediately, for two main reasons. Firstly, the Americans refused to act as a mere reinforcement, wishing instead to make their own individual contribu- tion to the air offensive. Secondly, they too had ideas about strategic bombing inherited from Mitchell and, secure in their development of the "self defending" bomber in the B-17 Flying Fortress and B-24 Liberator, refused to be dissuaded from delivering their attack upon Germany by daylight. Experiments had been carried out in California before the war which apparently proved that high-flying aircraft could hit extremely small targets with an impressive degree of success, and the Americans saw no reason to doubt that such results could also be achieved over Europe. Unfortunately, certain important problems had been overlooked, as the U.S. 8th Army Air Force found to its cost in 1942 and 1943.

The first of these was the weather. For high altitude precision attacks clear skies and good visibility were essential and, although such conditions may have been usual in California, they were conspicuously absent from the skies of North-West Europe for much of the year. The result was long periods during which no operations were possible or raids were aborted because of cloud cover over the target area, and this led to a dangerous undermining of crew morale, to say nothing of a lack of damage inflicted upon the enemy.

Secondly, and perhaps more importantly, the Cali- fornia experiments had taken no account of enemy opposition. If the skies were clear and visibility good

for the Americans, it was an ideal situation for the Germans too, for interceptors could attack the bombers with ease while the anti-aircraft guns needed only visual sightings. Needless to say, the initial American casualties were heavy, culminating in two raids on ball- bearings factories at Schweinfurt in 1943. In the first of these, on August 17, thirty-six bombers out of a force of 229 were lost, and when this was repeated on 14 October, with sixty out of 291 aircraft destroyed, the Americans were obliged to revise their ideas. As the majority of losses had been caused by the activity of interceptor fighters, despite the introduction of

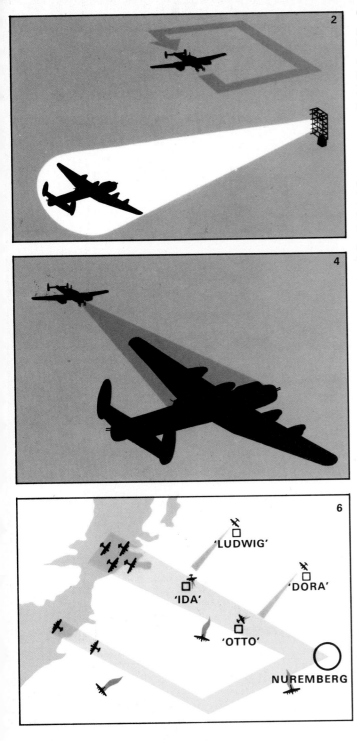

The pattern of radar interception. The chain of stations covered occupied Europe and Germany. They would first locate a bomber and vector in a circling night fighter. Once the fighter was within its own radar range it would attack. A typical raid on Nuremberg could catch the bomber stream on its approach to the target and as they returned home.

destroy the enemy aircraft one by one in the skies above Europe by mounting raids against almost anything that the Germans would be forced to defend. But the bombers could not do this alone, as the recent loss rates showed, and special long range escort fighters had to be developed. The use of escorts had never been expressly precluded from the American offensive, but in the early months the only available machines P-38 Lightnings, P-47 Thunderbolts, P-51 Allison-engined Mustangs and R.A.F. loaned Spitfires, lacked the range to escort bombers much beyond the borders of occupied France. It was not until late 1943 when Rolls-Royce engines were fitted into the Mustangs, that fighter aircraft appeared which could escort the bombers almost anywhere in Europe, engage the enemy and shoot him out of the sky. Then, and only then, did the Americans begin to gain the air superiority they so desperately needed.

With this American breakthrough on the one hand and the new British techniques of night bombing on the other, early 1944 should have seen the beginning of a true and decisive Combined Bomber Offensive, the orders for which had existed on paper since the Casablanca Conference and *Pointblank* Directive of January 1943. The Allied invasion of Europe took precedence, however, and between April and September 1944 the bulk of both bomber fleets was switched to tactical attacks upon the French Coast. Thus, when the strategic offensive began again in earnest in autumn 1944, the war was drawing to a close, and although the British and American bombers, flying by night and day respectively, were able to range far and wide over a rapidly-diminishing Germany for about eight months, it is arguable whether their offensive succeeded in the war-winning sense in which it had been undertaken.

The practical problems of mounting the type of air offensive envisaged in 1939 were immense for a start. On the British side it soon became apparent that Trenchard's belief in the impossibility of air defence was just not viable, and with loss rates of 50 per cent per operation experienced almost straight away, that the Royal Air Force's theory of daylight bombing needed revision. The subsequent switch from day to night bombing showed the problems of finding and destroying targets; the later switch from precision to area bombing necessitated the construction of an entirely new weapon. This took time and money – by the summer of 1943 some 40 per cent of British industrial effort was being devoted purely to the bomber offensive – and by the

"combat boxes" whereby the bombers grouped together for mutual protection, the only answer seemed to lie in the total destruction of the Luftwaffe. Until it had been lured out and destroyed, the daylight offensive could not even begin for, regardless of Mitchell's belief and the California experiments, the self-defending bomber needed complete air superiority to be effective.

The obvious method of achieving this superiority was to destroy the Luftwaffe and its support services on the ground by attacking airfields, oil installations and aircraft factories, but the casualty figures in the process were sure to be high. The Americans chose instead to time that Bomber Command was ready to wage an effective air offensive, the tactical demands of D-Day had taken precedence. The same thing happened with the Americans, for the practical problems of gaining complete air supremacy delayed the development of their offensive to its full potential. The overall result of these problems and delays was that in a war lasting nearly six years, full scale strategic bombing could only be carried out for about eight months. So strategic bombing, far from being the straightforward operation that the inter-war theorists imagined, was in fact a highly complicated affair, necessitating the devotion of huge amounts of money and scientific knowledge even to begin. When it is remembered that by May 1945 nearly 100,000 Allied airmen had lost their lives one begins to ask whether it was all worth the effort.

These doubts are reinforced when, as a second factor, the physical results of the offensive upon Germany are examined. Going back to the original theory, the offensive had two aims – the undermining of civilian morale and the destruction of German war industry – and, although the methods employed by the Allies were altered, these remained the aims throughout. Were they achieved?

So far as civilian morale was concerned, the answer must be no. Isolated examples of panic may be found – for example, the Hamburg fire-storm of July 1943 caused 900,000 people to flee the area and spread alarm but, overall, bombing had the same effect upon Germany as it had upon Britain in 1940/41: that is it caused a determination to carry on and work together in the face of common adversity. In Germany, of course, the process was aided by a repressive Nazi regime, imposing an iron rule which, if broken, resulted in punishment worse than aerial bombardment.

It is far more difficult to draw any conclusion concerning the effects of bombing upon German war industry. There is no doubt that the Allies grossly underestimated German industrial potential throughout the war. Thus, although attacks might destroy an industrial plant, it tended to be out of action for a comparatively short time as the machinery and workers could either be quickly replaced or moved elsewhere. In addition, German industry was mobilized only gradually, in step with military efforts, and it is a fact that by 1944 German war production was running at a higher level than in 1940, before the bomber offensive began; a fact which may be appreciated from the following table:

German War-Material Output 1940-1944

	1940	1941	1942	1943	1944
Aircraft	10,200	11,000	14,200	25,000	39,600
Tanks	1,600	3,800	6,300	12,100	19,000
Artillery	6,300	7,800	13,600	38,000	62,300
Ammunition (Million rounds)	2,950	1,340	1,340	3,170	5,370
U-Boats	76	218	238	279	229
Oil (1,000 met. tons)	4,652	5,542	6,368	7,508	5,412

On this evidence it would appear that the bombing failed to contribute a great deal to the winning of the war.

This is perhaps an extreme view, for a number of other factors do need to be considered. Firstly, there is of course no saying what tremendous heights of war-production would have been achieved by Germany if bombing had not taken place. Secondly, as a result of the bombing, by 1943 German industrial output had been forced on to the defensive, to manufacture defensive weapons and aircraft instead of tanks and artillery. Similarly, by early 1944, 1,000,000 trained soldiers and airmen were tied down in Germany itself manning anti-aircraft defences, and many Luftwaffe squadrons were committed to air defence instead of tactical attacks upon enemy armies. Their effect alone upon either the Western or Eastern Fronts could have been decisive.

These points undoubtedly balance the picture, but the question must still remain: Was it all worthwhile? Obviously, if the war had been won by the bombing offensive alone, one would have no hesitation in applauding the perspicacity of men like Douhet, Mitchell and Trenchard, but it must be remembered and emphasized that it was the physical defeat of German armies and occupation of German territory by Allied land forces which brought the war to an end. Strategic bombing undoubtedly weakened German strength and contributed to the final victory, but taking all the evidence together, the theory of strategic bombing as a war-winner, put forward in 1939, did not fulfil its promise. Not only did the methods by which it was to be executed need radical alteration in the face of practical problems, but the aims themselves were grossly overestimated. On the evidence of the offensive against Germany, air power did not have a strategic viability in the war winning sense.

But this view is based upon the results of one cam-

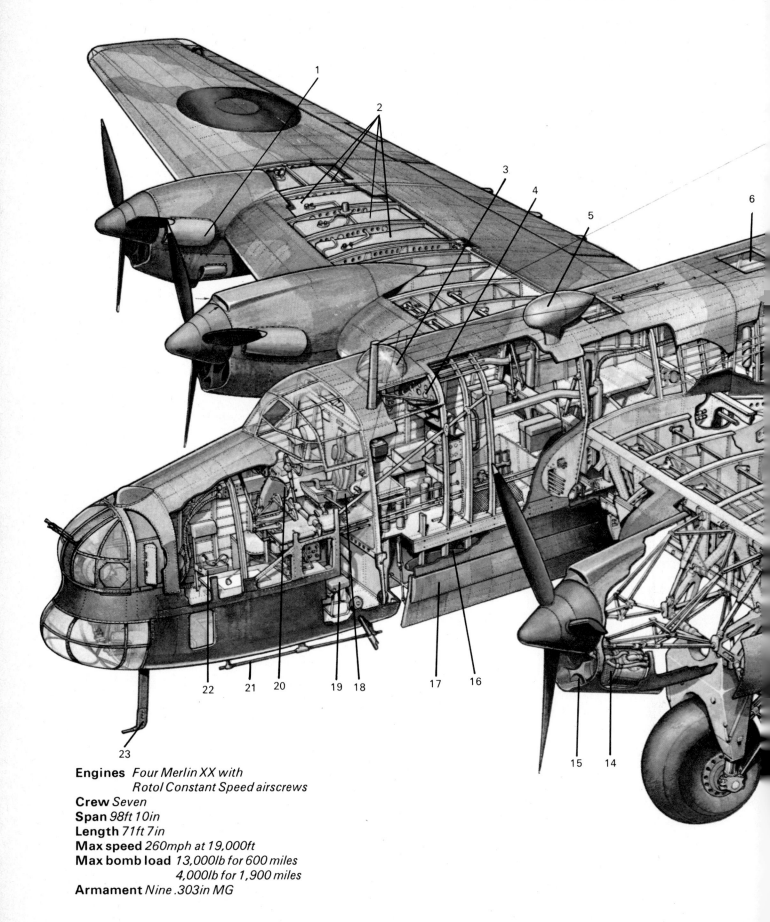

Engines *Four Merlin XX with*
Rotol Constant Speed airscrews
Crew *Seven*
Span *98ft 10in*
Length *71ft 7in*
Max speed *260mph at 19,000ft*
Max bomb load *13,000lb for 600 miles*
4,000lb for 1,900 miles
Armament *Nine .303in MG*

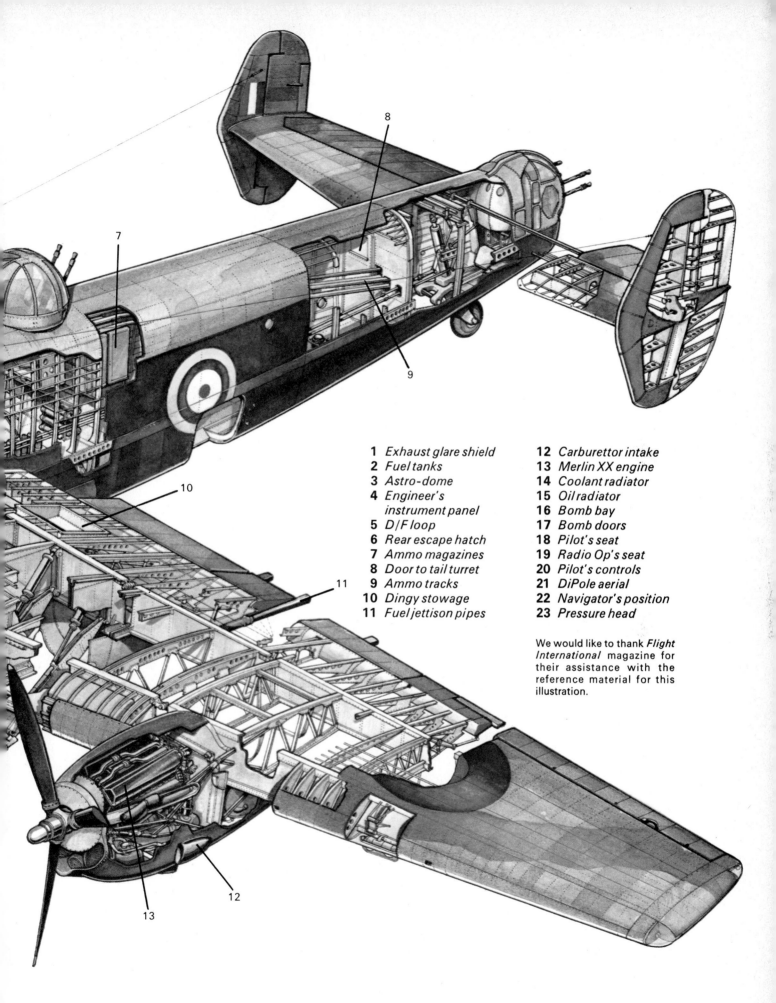

1 Exhaust glare shield
2 Fuel tanks
3 Astro-dome
4 Engineer's instrument panel
5 D/F loop
6 Rear escape hatch
7 Ammo magazines
8 Door to tail turret
9 Ammo tracks
10 Dingy stowage
11 Fuel jettison pipes
12 Carburettor intake
13 Merlin XX engine
14 Coolant radiator
15 Oil radiator
16 Bomb bay
17 Bomb doors
18 Pilot's seat
19 Radio Op's seat
20 Pilot's controls
21 DiPole aerial
22 Navigator's position
23 Pressure head

We would like to thank *Flight International* magazine for their assistance with the reference material for this illustration.

paign only, and in order to reach as balanced a conclusion as possible, it is necessary to examine, in
general terms at least, the lessons of the offensives
against Japan and North Vietnam.

Taking them in order, the Japanese declaration of
war on America by attacking Pearl Harbour on 7
December 1941, found the American air forces, despite
the influence of Mitchell's ideas, unprepared for an
immediate strategic offensive. Plans for attacking the
Japanese homeland existed on paper but, when it came
to putting these into practice, a multiplicity of problems arose.

The most important of these was a complete lack of
suitable bases from which to send the bombers for,
with Japanese advances through the Pacific in early
1942, all the islands capable of maintaining airstrips
within range of Japan had been lost. The only alternative was mainland China, where Chiang Kai-shek's
armies had been fighting the Japanese since 1937, but
once again the practical difficulties were awesome. So
long as Japanese forces remained in the area, any
airfields in China were in constant danger of being
over-run, while the long and tenuous supply line over
the Himalayas from India made the maintenance of a
bomber fleet virtually impossible. Admittedly, as early
as April 18 1942 Colonel James Doolittle did lead a
raid on Tokyo with B-25 Mitchell bombers flown from
the aircraft-carrier, *Hornet*, but this was never regarded
as a long-term answer to the problem and may be
seen purely as an exercise in American morale-boosting.
An immense amount of organization was clearly needed
before a true strategic offensive could be launched.

In the event, despite the disadvantages, the Americans
chose to base their bombers initially in China, and it
was from there that the specially designed B-29 Super-
fortress long-range aircraft began the assault upon
Japan. But the first raids did not take place until June
1944, two and a half years after the outbreak of war,
and even then were not particularly effective. Carrying
out daylight precision attacks according to the Mitchell
theory, the B-29s suffered heavy losses, chiefly because
they had to cross so much Japanese-occupied territory
before approaching their targets, and on a number of
occasions the raids ceased altogether because of
Japanese attacks upon forward air bases, a lack of
supplies coming through from India, or most common
of all, the atrocious weather conditions. It was not until
the Americans had retaken the Marianas Islands in the
Central Pacific that a relatively secure base became

available. And as that campaign did not end until
August 1944, the islands could not be prepared to
receive the B-29s until the following November.

As a result, however, the China-based operations
were gradually phased out, and from December 1944
the offensive began in earnest from the Marianas. By
that time tactics had changed dramatically, in much the
same way as those of the Royal Air Force had changed
during the early months of the offensive against
Germany. By the end of 1944 it was more common for
the B-29s to indulge in area bombing – with incendiaries and the newly-invented napalm being
dropped on to Japanese houses rather than factories –
and not unknown for the raids to take place at night.
The use of these techniques culminated in the

A USAAF B-29 over its target. Though the bomb-load was not as great as the RAF Lancaster, the B-29 was pressurized which enabled the crew to take it out of range of anti-aircraft fire from the ground. Below: USAAF B-17s escorted by Mustangs form up over England prior to a daylight raid on Germany.

devastating fire-raid on Tokyo during the night of March 9/10 1945 in which, it is estimated, nearly a quarter of a million people died. So far as destructive capability was concerned, the tactics of the offensive could not be faulted but, once again, the strategy of ending the war through such raids did not work. The Japanese people did not panic and their industries, although badly affected, did not cease production. In other words, the lessons of this offensive would appear to be the same as those of the offensive against Germany: the mounting of a strategic bombing campaign is time-consuming, costly and fraught with problems; that the bomber does not always get through to hit precision targets by daylight, necessitating a switch to night-time area bombing to counteract losses

and a lack of results, and that, even then, civilian panic and the destruction of the enemy's war-industry does not necessarily follow.

But this was not the end of the story so far as the offensive against Japan was concerned, for on 6 and 9 August 1945 the Americans dropped atomic bombs on Hiroshima and Nagasaki respectively. The results of these attacks were immediately applauded as complete vindications of the theories of Douhet and Mitchell, for by dropping the atomic bombs a Japanese surrender was achieved and an extremely costly seaborne invasion of Japan averted. Arguments for the continued existence of air forces on a strategic level received a much-needed boost and, in the American case, led to the formation of an independent Strategic Air Command, charged solely with the delivery of atomic weapons. Indeed, some theorists in America even went so far as to suggest that, with such weapons available, there was little need for large conventional ground and sea forces: an interesting reversion to one of the more controversial arguments of Douhet and Mitchell.

Unfortunately, for the Americans, the Russians developed their own atomic bombs in 1949 and, with the realization that a strategic offensive involving such weapons would result in retaliation and an unacceptable amount of damage to both sides, atomic warfare entered the realms of deterrence, with neither superpower prepared to attack the other except under the type of provocation which has yet to appear. Nevertheless, as a direct result of the attacks upon Hiroshima and Nagasaki, it became widely accepted that strategic bombing could be a war-winner, without any differentiation being made between conventional and atomic weaponry. Despite the glaring lessons of the Second World War, it was argued once again that the decisive element was the air and widely believed that a strategic bombing offensive, regardless of the weapons used, could decide a future war without a great deal of dependence upon military or naval campaigns. The results of this interesting exercise in ignoring the lessons of the past is illustrated in Vietnam, particularly in the American attacks upon North Vietnam between February 1965 and February 1973.

Dispassionate and accurate information about these engagements is hard to find since we are fairly close to the event, but it is apparent that when they began in 1965 there were three basic aims. Firstly, to impede North Vietnamese infiltration into the south by hitting supply lines, bridges and rear areas north of the Demilitarized Zone around the 17th Parallel: a campaign more of tactical interdiction than strategic consequence. Secondly, it was foreseen that any raids upon the enemy would help raise the flagging morale of the South Vietnamese and it was later also seen as a boost to the morale of the American ground forces, but this too could hardly be described as strategic. Thirdly, and more importantly, it was argued that through a strategy of precision attacks upon key industries – petroleum, lubricants, hydro-electric power plants, coal, iron and steel – the Hanoi Government would be forced to sue for peace or at least to stop supporting the Viet Cong in the South. Moreover, this strategy was to include an element of "punitive bargaining", whereby the Americans in their aptly

named *Rolling Thunder* operations, would begin by attacking rural-based industries to show the capability of their air-power. This, it was hoped, would cause the North Vietnamese to stop and reflect upon their position. If that did not work, the next series of attacks would approach nearer to the cities of Hanoi and Haiphong before another pause gave the enemy one more chance to see the error of his ways. At all times, the emphasis was to be firmly upon the precise destruction of key industries, but in effect the Americans were holding the cities of North Vietnam hostage, subject to Hanoi's decision about the continuation of the conflict.

This was perhaps a rather vain hope, as one imagines any World War II bombing veteran could have pointed out, and was not really argued through to its logical conclusion. The American policy-makers in Washington do not appear to have contemplated what would happen once the strategic bombers and their escorts had reached Hanoi and Haiphong, and in the event the results were predictable. By 1973 the Americans had dropped ten times the weight of bombs on North Vietnam than had been dropped throughout the Second World War on Germany and Japan together, and were actually attacking targets within the urban centres, all to little avail. America came under intense pressure both from other World powers and from domestic opinion to stop the offensive entirely; fighter bombers were shot down by surface-to-air missiles and ground fire, and the crews who survived became useful hostages to the enemy in the eventual peace negotiations; the North Vietnamese did not panic and, as they possessed no real war industries, being supplied in large measure from other Communist states, felt few effects in front-line units. Moreover, on occasions the accuracy of the offensive left much to be desired (as the inhabitants of the Algerian Embassy in Hanoi – situated over a mile away from the nearest industrial target – found to their cost in 1970) and the North Vietnamese were bombed neither to the conference table nor "back into the Stone Age". Once again the lesson, which should by now have been apparent, had to be learned the hard way: strategic bombing, using conventional weapons, does not win wars.

This basically, stands as the main conclusion, although it does not mean that the theory of strategic bombing is entirely dead: far from it. Both America and the Soviet Union – who are about the only countries still able to afford strategic equipment on a large-scale

A cutaway view of the
U-235 bomb 'Little Boy'.
U-235
 1. Tail cone
 2. Stabilizing tail fins
 3. Airstream defectors
 4. Air inlet tube
 5. Pressure sensors
 6. Packing
 7. Electronic conduits and
    fusing circuits
 8. Neutron reflector
 9. Cast bomb casing
10. Lead shield container
11. Fuses
12. Telemetry monitoring probes
13. Battery stores
14. Conventional explosive
    charge
15. Detonating head
16. Airstream deflectors
17. Air pressure detonator

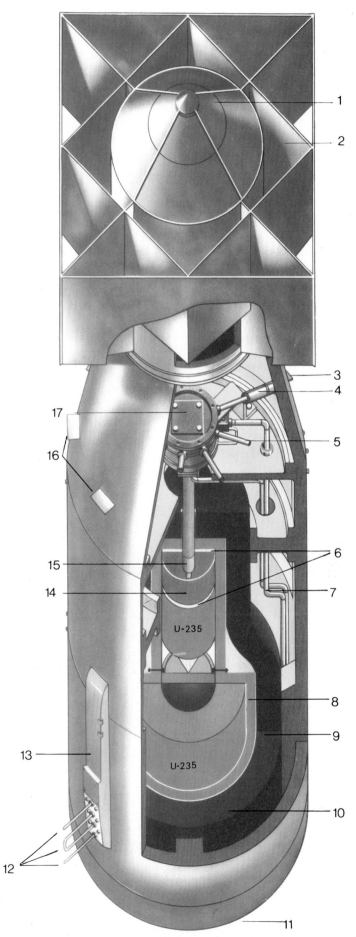

– are currently involved in the development and manufacture of weapons aimed specifically at undermining, through the element of the air, the enemy's moral and physical capability to wage effective war. Admittedly the majority of these weapons are nuclear and as such, because of their devastating power, may indeed be vindications of the theories of Douhet and Mitchell, but it is interesting to note that the use of conventional ordnance, delivered by the manned bomber, is not ignored. On the Soviet side, the Backfire bomber has been produced in fairly large numbers for both nuclear and conventional delivery, and although its makers state that it has the range for only tactical strikes within the European theatre, it could be equipped with refuelling facilities which would enable it to reach the eastern seaboard of America. Meanwhile the Americans, despite their recent cancellation of the B-1 bomber, are maintaining a substantial fleet of up-dated B-52s, primarily as delivery platforms for the revolutionary Air-Launched Cruise Missile (ALCM).

These ALCMs with their sophisticated contour-matching guidance systems, enabling them to "read" the ground over which they are flying, are able to approach their chosen targets at altitudes of less than 100 feet, below the radar and anti-aircraft defensive cover, and are accurate to within thirty feet over 2000 miles. They are undoubtedly the weapons of the future, and it can be argued that they alter the entire complexion of strategic bombing. They represent the latest outcome of a technological revolution which began during the Vietnam War, when the Americans developed "smart" bombs, guided by television cameras or laser beams on to specific targets: a development which seemed at last to solve the constant problem of bombing accuracy, so making the bombing of selected industrial targets more effective. Certainly, when such weapons were field-tested against oil-installations near Hanoi in 1972 the results were impressive, but they are expensive and may be susceptible to Electronic Counter-Measures (ECM). In addition, in any future war, particularly between the superpowers, they will probably be used against tactical targets only. If war reaches strategic level, nuclear warheads can do the job of destruction so much better, and if they are used, strategic bombing may well be so devastating that arguments about its effectiveness would be meaningless. In short, strategic bombing can only work if the devastation is so enormous that results are virtually instantaneous.

Reconnaissance and observation

16 FISHBEDS

2 FAGOTS

An airfield in Cuba with Soviet-built fighters on dispersal points along the main strip.

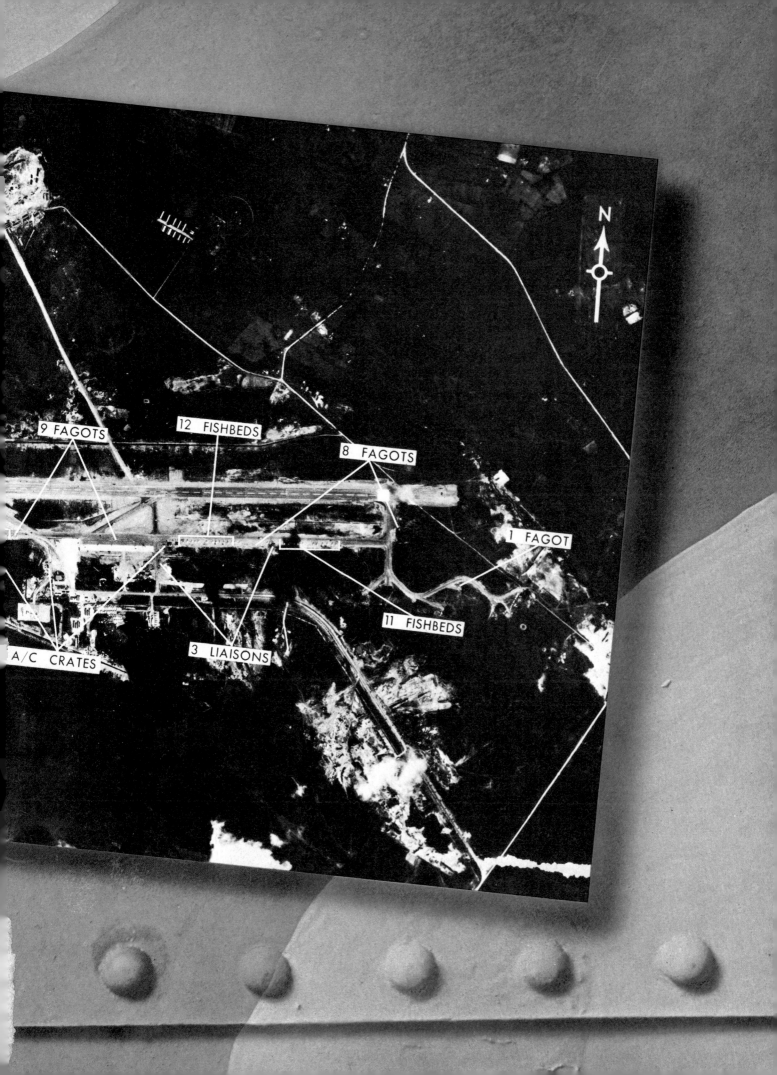

Despite the rather negative conclusions reached so far, there can be little doubt that air power has revolutionized warfare during the present century, chiefly by adding a third dimension which offers entirely new concepts and capabilities to those involved in the management of organized conflict. The fact that the strategic potential of these capabilities was exaggerated in the past does not lessen the impact of air power, and it is the aim of this part of the book to analyze that impact in the tactical, or battlefield, areas of war.

The most obvious military use of aircraft when they first appeared was in the role of reconnaissance /observation. One of the basic principles of successful warfare is the element of surprise and to achieve it at times and places of your own choosing, it is necessary to know as much about the enemy as possible. Before the advent of aircraft, such reconnaissance and observation had to be carried out by spies or by elements of the army or navy acting well in advance of the main force. During the Peninsula War (1808-14) for example, the Duke of Wellington used both methods, sending out spies behind the French lines to sketch out enemy dispositions and to assess possible routes of march for the main army, and using his cavalry units to report on the situation "on the other side of the hill." In a naval context, and taking the same period of history, Lord Nelson substituted merchant sailors for spies and fast frigates or gun-boats for cavalry. But, in all cases, the results were poor. Information was restricted to the immediate area observed by a few men only; what they saw was subject to geography and terrain on a two-dimensional setting; and by the time their intelligence had been relayed to the commander, it was invariably out of date. The introduction of aircraft which could fly relatively quickly over long distances over the top of natural obstacles changed all this and the reconnaissance/observation potential was soon appreciated. It was given credibility on its way to becoming an integral part of military organization by a tradition of experimentation with balloons which had been going on since at least 1794 when, at the Battle of Fleurus, the French observed enemy positions and altered their scheme of attack accordingly. Indeed, by the time of the Wrights' experiments in 1903 most European armies (and some navies) had balloon sections, but use of the balloon was restricted by its dependence upon calm conditions and attachment, by static lines, to one point on the ground. Balloon observers were useless in a fluid battle situation.

It was Captain Piazza of the Italian air service who gave the first intimation of the new potential over Tripoli in 1911, although many refused at first to accept his claims of success. Some of the more reactionary generals, not only in Italy but elsewhere, even went so far as to doubt whether anything distinct could be seen by someone flying above the ground at fifty miles an hour. Nowhere was this more apparent than in the British Army, where the tradition-conscious cavalry regarded the aircraft as a rival for one of their most coveted roles. But as early as 1912 even they were forced to accept the new weapon, for in the army manoeuvres of that year elements of the fledgling Royal Flying Corps changed the course of the mock battle. Trenchard, the new recruit to the Corps, flew as an observer for the northern force under General Grierson, with orders to locate General Haig's advancing southern force. This he did, reporting back to Grierson within an hour of take-off and reinforcing the lesson by then acting as an aerial messenger to Grierson's cavalry force, recalling it from a false advance, to counter Haig's attack. Afterwards it was admitted officially that the success enjoyed by Grierson had been largely influenced by the "intervention of aircraft" and, as the air historian Sir Walter Raleigh later wrote, "the aeroplanes rose to such esteem that they were asked to verify information which had been brought in by the cavalry."

With evidence like this available, it was hardly surprising that, in 1914, reconnaissance and observation was an accepted role for aircraft. In fact, however, the First World War saw little dramatic development in this area. While the land campaigns, especially on the Western Front, remained fluid, the great potential was recognized, and there is evidence to suggest that during the Allied retreat from Mons in September 1914 French and British air observers contributed to a relative lack of confusion by keeping commanders informed about the situation on the ground. Once the trench deadlock set in after December 1914, however, air reconnaissance/observation was affected by two important factors. Firstly, since the armies were static, it was not so necessary to assess enemy dispositions over a wide area, and this enabled the balloon to re-appear in an observation role at the front line. Aircraft still contributed, chiefly in the areas of deep reconnaissance and artillery spotting, but as an enemy build-up could usually be both seen and heard by ground forces in the trenches, much of the preparatory

work laid down by people such as Piazza and Trenchard was invalidated under the prevailing circumstances.

This was emphasized still further by the second, related development, for it did not take long for both sides to realize that it was possible and, of course, desirable, to blind the enemy by depriving him of his observation aircraft and balloons. There quickly developed the concept of the interceptor, or fighter aircraft, armed with machine-guns, which could shoot enemy reconnaissance/observation machines out of the sky before they could report what they had seen. Rather than risk losing such a valuable source of information in this way, it became usual for reconnaissance aircraft and observation balloons to be protected from the fighters – and what better weapon than another fighter? By 1916 it had become normal for all reconnaissance/observation missions to be protected and for air-to-air combat between protecting and attacking fighters to take place. The famous "dog-fights" of the First World War were the result, and this constant battle for air supremacy – defined at the time as the ability to observe the enemy from the air without fear of attack or destruction – continued right up to 1918. It constituted one of the most important tactical lessons of World War I – if air reconnaissance/ observation is to be successful, you must have the

ability to use the skies as and when you deem necessary, not merely when the enemy permits. The difficulties encountered as enemy counter-measures became more effective tended to relegate this role to one of only secondary importance, the prime necessity being the achievement and maintenance of air superiority.

Such a decline in importance was reflected in the relative lack of emphasis placed upon reconnaissance/ observation between the two World Wars. The previously mentioned air power theorists virtually dismissed the idea as irrelevant to the more essential needs of strategic bombing, and few air forces devoted much time or effort to the development of skills beyond the level which had prevailed before 1914. But as the Second World War approached, air technology began to provide at least the basics for improvements in the reconnaissance and observation areas. The first and most important of these lay in the evolution of aircraft, principally for racing and the achievement of endurance and air-speed records. No longer would air observers be expected to hover around at fifty or seventy-five miles an hour, as in World War I, they could now streak over the area to be reconnoitred at three or four hundred miles an hour, surprising ground defences and standing a fair chance of outstripping opposing interceptors. In addition, they were no longer restricted to the lower

When de Havillands proposed a twin-engined bomber made of wood, the British Air Ministry were incredulous. But it worked. In operation, the versatile Mosquito was a major factor in winning the war in the air between 1939 and 1945. In no fewer than 43 Marks, from PR, bomber, trainer, day and night fighter, intruder, ground-attack, anti-shipping, torpedo-reconnaissance, the well-behaved 'Mossie' carried out every operational task allotted it with devastating efficiency.

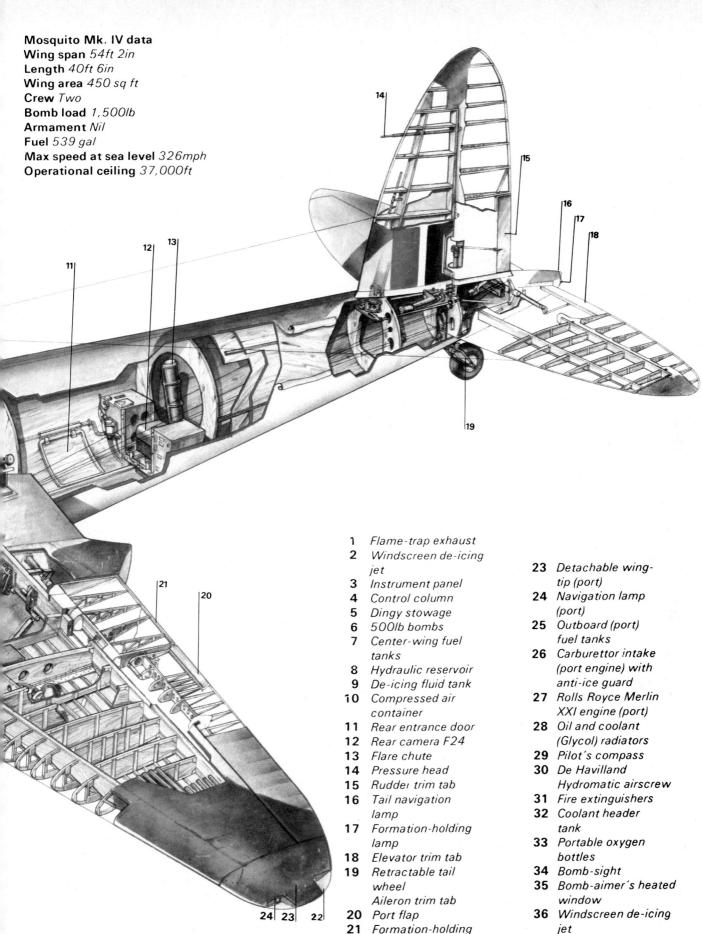

Mosquito Mk. IV data
Wing span *54ft 2in*
Length *40ft 6in*
Wing area *450 sq ft*
Crew *Two*
Bomb load *1,500lb*
Armament *Nil*
Fuel *539 gal*
Max speed at sea level *326mph*
Operational ceiling *37,000ft*

1   *Flame-trap exhaust*
2   *Windscreen de-icing jet*
3   *Instrument panel*
4   *Control column*
5   *Dingy stowage*
6   *500lb bombs*
7   *Center-wing fuel tanks*
8   *Hydraulic reservoir*
9   *De-icing fluid tank*
10 *Compressed air container*
11 *Rear entrance door*
12 *Rear camera F24*
13 *Flare chute*
14 *Pressure head*
15 *Rudder trim tab*
16 *Tail navigation lamp*
17 *Formation-holding lamp*
18 *Elevator trim tab*
19 *Retractable tail wheel*
    Aileron trim tab
20 *Port flap*
21 *Formation-holding*
22 *lamp (port)*

23 *Detachable wing-tip (port)*
24 *Navigation lamp (port)*
25 *Outboard (port) fuel tanks*
26 *Carburettor intake (port engine) with anti-ice guard*
27 *Rolls Royce Merlin XXI engine (port)*
28 *Oil and coolant (Glycol) radiators*
29 *Pilot's compass*
30 *De Havilland Hydromatic airscrew*
31 *Fire extinguishers*
32 *Coolant header tank*
33 *Portable oxygen bottles*
34 *Bomb-sight*
35 *Bomb-aimer's heated window*
36 *Windscreen de-icing jet*
37 *Air thermometer*

reaches of the sky, but could now soar upwards to altitudes outside the effective range of anti-aircraft guns and could, conceivably, come and go before the enemy realized what was happening. This clearly made air reconnaissance and observation a more viable operation, but the argument that little of value could be seen from the air naturally re-appeared; after all, the higher you fly and the faster you move, the less intelligence you are going to gain.

This is where the second technological development came in – the reliable air-photo camera. Pictures had been taken from aircraft since the earliest days – indeed many of the impressions we now have of First World War trench-systems snaking across a devastated landscape come from air-photos. But obviously the faster and higher you flew, the less clear these became. Moreover, in the early days, when speed and height were not essential, each aircraft could carry an observer in addition to the pilot, who leant over the side to take the relevant photographs. However as aircraft became faster they needed to lose weight, or at least concentrate it in a more powerful engine, and this meant losing the observer. No pilot could be expected to fly and photograph at the same time so the development of remotely-controlled cameras, attached to a firm base within the aircraft, was clearly a breakthrough of some importance. Allied to this was a growth in the ability to decipher and interpret exactly what the photograph contained, so that by 1939 aerial reconnaissance/observation was a well equipped, established part of air warfare.

Examples of the successful appplication of this role during the Second World War are many and varied. On the Allied side the Royal Air Force kept a careful watch upon German barge concentrations in the coastal ports of France and the Low Countries during the *Sea Lion* invasion scare of late 1940. They also contributed to a significant extent in the strategic bombing campaign of 1939-45 by observing weather patterns over Germany and assessing the damage done once the raids had been delivered. During the build-up to, and the actual execution of the D-Day invasion of Europe in June 1944, air reconnaissance provided vital information about enemy defences, troop dispositions and movements, and this was continued as the Allied armies pushed on towards Germany. In other spheres, it was air reconnaissance that first pin-pointed the German development of V-weapons at Peenemunde on the Baltic coast in 1943, and later helped to identify the sites in Northern France from which the revolutionary VI ("Doodlebug") pilotless bombs were launched: a factor which contributed in no small way to the Allied decision to advance northwards to take out these sites rather than directly eastwards towards the centre of Germany. Indeed on all fronts, both Allied and Axis, many military decisions were taken purely on the basis of information from air photographs.

But perhaps the most dramatic examples of success in this role came at sea. Certainly so far as Britain was concerned, during the period up to 1943 the life-line with America was all-important and the battle against the U-boats and German surface raiders became an essential one to win as quickly as possible. Unfortunately submarines and single surface vessels are extremely difficult to find once they are at sea, so air observation of their ports, supply points and routes is obviously vital. During the battle of the Atlantic (1939-43), aircraft contributed in no small measure to the final Allied victory, and although their more aggressive roles will be dealt with later, their ability to keep track of enemy vessels does need to be mentioned now. When the German surface fleet began to show signs of activity, for example – a development apparent from as early as 1939 when the battleship *Graf Spee* appeared in the South Atlantic – aircraft were dispatched to maintain round-the-clock watches on known or possible anchorages. The results were impressive. When the battleship *Bismarck* escaped into the North Atlantic in 1941, it was reconnaissance aircraft from Britain which traced her to an obscure Norwegian fjord and provided the first steps in her eventual pursuit and destruction. Similarly when *Tirpitz* tried to follow her sister-ship a year later, air reconnaissance was so effective that she was kept under observation so closely that she found it impossible to move out of Norway without elements of the Royal Navy showing an immediate and unhealthy knowledge of her exact whereabouts. The same degree of success was achieved when it came to finding U-boat bases and directing bombing raids against them, so that overall the contribution of air reconnaissance/observation to this battle alone suggests a substantial restoration to its former primacy. Specially adapted Spitfires, devoid of all unnecessary weight, and the extra-light Mosquitoes, constructed almost entirely of plywood, showed that by flying fast and high the First World War problems of ground fire and interception in the air could be successfully overcome.

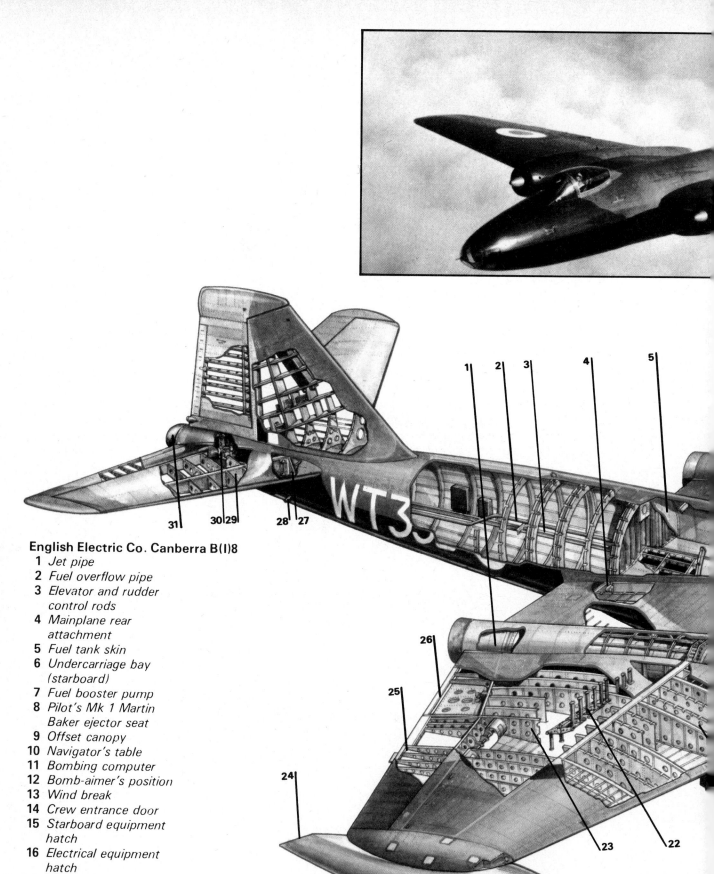

English Electric Co. Canberra B(I)8

1 Jet pipe
2 Fuel overflow pipe
3 Elevator and rudder
  control rods
4 Mainplane rear
  attachment
5 Fuel tank skin
6 Undercarriage bay
  (starboard)
7 Fuel booster pump
8 Pilot's Mk 1 Martin
  Baker ejector seat
9 Offset canopy
10 Navigator's table
11 Bombing computer
12 Bomb-aimer's position
13 Wind break
14 Crew entrance door
15 Starboard equipment
   hatch
16 Electrical equipment
   hatch
17 Bomb bay doors
18 Bomb bay
19 Triple breech starter

The English Electric Canberra B(I)8 was the night-intruder interdictor version of an aircraft which underwent a series of modifications and variant-types for 26 years, culminating in a number of one-offs for investigation into electronic counter-measures. Introduced in July 1954, the B(I)8, with a wing-span of 63ft 11½in, was 65ft 6in long and was powered by two Avon 109 turbojets each producing 7,500lb of thrust. The pilot sat in a cockpit off-set to port under a canopy which gave increased visibility. Access was through a hatch on the starboard side of the nose. Navigator/bomb-aimer/radio operator sat in the nose section. There was provision for 6,000lb of bombs in the bomb-bay and wing-racks. Top speed was in the region of 580mph. It was produced for the 2nd Tactical Airforce to deliver nuclear weapons and had a low-altitude bomb-sight.

20 Rolls Royce Avon 109 turbojet
21 Integral fuel tanks
22 Air-brake drag channels
23 Mainplane structure
24 Jettisonable fuel tank
25 Aileron, starboard
26 Flap, starboard
27 Tailplane hinges
28 Fuel overflow pipe
29 Tailplane structure
30 Tailplane actuator
31 Tail-cone

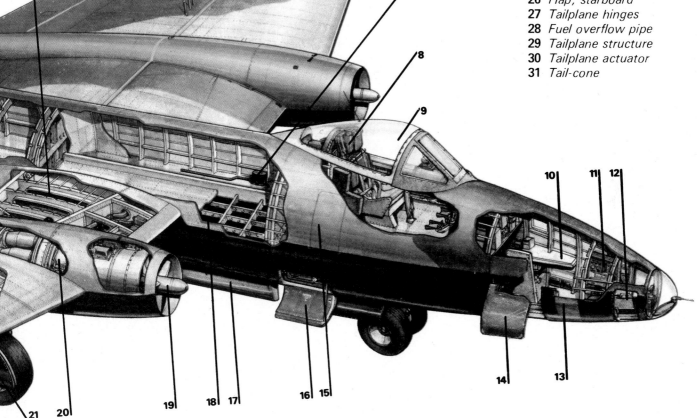

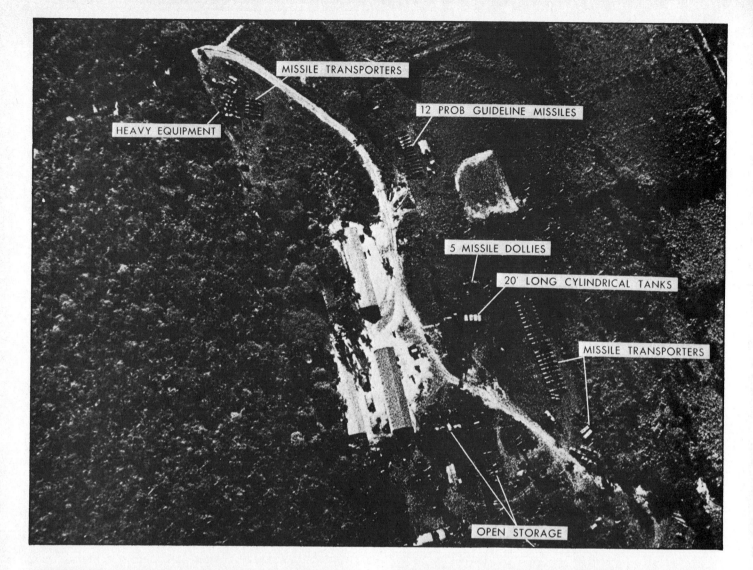

MISSILE TRANSPORTERS

HEAVY EQUIPMENT

12 PROB GUIDELINE MISSILES

5 MISSILE DOLLIES

20' LONG CYLINDRICAL TANKS

MISSILE TRANSPORTERS

OPEN STORAGE

Left: One of the reconnaissance photographs of Cuba that triggered the Cuban Missile Crisis of October 1962. The missiles and equipment have been indicated for distribution to the Press.
Below left: An industrial target before and after an attack by the USAAF in World War II.
Right: An RPV, Remotely Piloted Vehicle, a pilotless reconnaissance drone which is difficult to locate on radar and relatively expendable.

Viewing the situation since 1945, it is impossible to conclude anything but a mammoth expansion in this area. This is partly a result of the Cold War and superpower confrontation which has characterized the nuclear age, for in such circumstances of wary, but non-violent, hostility, information about the potential enemy, his dispositions and possible intentions, is clearly essential. But this does not alter the fact that the massive technological leaps which have occurred since the Second World War have made the whole area of reconnaissance/observation much more effective. To take an extreme example, the existence of special spy-satellites capable, through infra-red photography, of taking detailed pictures of the earth from beyond the atmosphere, obviously take the lid off not only the battlefield but also the most inaccessible areas of the enemy homeland. This is particularly useful in the context of superpower dentente and arms limitation, for in the absence of information freely provided by either side such things as missile sites, ABM (anti-ballistic missile) complexes and submarine pens can be checked by air reconnaissance. The satellites are also less dangerous than aircraft for, as the U-2 crisis in 1960 illustrated (when the American pilot Gary Powers was shot down over Russia), it can be very embarrassing to be caught in the act of aerial reconnaissance during peacetime. In addition, satellites enable the two super powers to maintain a careful watch upon potential or actual trouble-spots around the world and advise any of their allies who may be involved of the true situation. This was shown to good effect during the Arab-Israeli War of 1973, for it was spy-satellite pictures, provided by the Russians, which showed President Sadat of Egypt the true extent of Israeli gains on the west bank of the Suez Canal just before the cease-fire agreement of October 22. Sadat could never have gathered such information from the confused situation on the ground, yet he needed it desperately in order to decide upon the advisability of the cease-fire.

But spy-satellites are an extreme example and in the event of a major war between the super powers they are likely to be blotted out almost straight away: both sides are reported to have contingency plans which even include sending astronauts into space to steal the enemy's equipment! If this is the case, aircraft are sure to return to the reconnaissance/observation role, and neither super power has neglected the development of reconnaissance machines, concentrating as before upon speed and altitude. The latest American contribution – the aptly named Blackbird – now holds the trans-Atlantic speed record, while the Soviet Tu-20 Bear is a constant visitor to the shores of Britain and Western Europe, probing air defence systems and monitoring radar wave-lengths for future jamming or ECM, should a war occur. In addition, both sides have developed multi-role aircraft which will be expected, as a part of their job, to do reconnaissance sweeps over the battle area itself.

Before leaving this role, however, it is worth considering the latest developments in the reconnaissance sphere. During the Vietnam War the Americans were presented with the problem of keeping a constant watch upon possible infiltration and supply routes into the south, particularly around the Demilitarized Zone and on the Laotian and Cambodian borders. At first they used the traditional means of reconnaissance aircraft, equipped with such technological innovations as infra-red cameras, electronic surveillance devices and even "people-sniffers" (small dart-like objects dropped into the jungle and capable of warning the pilot of human movement through a sensitivity to body heat and odour), later the idea of Remotely Piloted Vehicles (RPVs) was put forward. These aircraft contained all the equipment used by conventional reconnaissance aircraft, but relayed their findings by television and radar to a secure ground controller, were expendable, relatively cheap and, of course, pilotless; considerations which soon led to their extension into the tactical strike and even bombing roles. So far as reconnaissance/observation is concerned, however, they are now in front-line use – according to newspaper reports of July 1977, a number were shot down by the Libyans during their border war with Egypt – and are quite clearly the equipment of the future. The amount of money and research still being devoted to such developments shows how important the basic role of reconnaissance/observation is, and implies its continuation for as long as the air is used for military purposes.

Tactical support and Interdiction

Bombing up a Hawker Hurricane IIc in North Africa.
When the Hurricane became too slow to be an interceptor it proved an excellent ground attack fighter.

Early experiments in what later came be to known as
tactical strike support coincided with those on recon-
naissance/observation, when the Italians under Piazza,
dropped small bombs on the Turkish camps around
Tripoli in 1911 at the same time as they were observing
dispositions and force levels. This was only logical,
obeying the military maxim of attacking the enemy
wherever he may be found, and immediately offered a
new and important role to the aircraft. So far as
military forces are concerned, any preliminary attacks
upon an enemy, demoralizing his troops, cutting his
immediate lines of communication or supply (a process
now known as interdiction), disrupting his movement
of reinforcements and destroying his more static
elements such as airfields, railheads, artillery positions
and troop concentrations, are extremely beneficial. They
will weaken an attacking force by blunting his assault,
or they will prepare the way for an advance by undermining enemy strength and efficiency. If, in addition,
the strikes are maintained as the battle develops, then
the side with the strongest air element will clearly enjoy
a substantial advantage.

There was obviously nothing new about the
principles behind this role – it had long been a basic
task of the army artillery – but the extension of it to
aircraft was soon accepted. As with so many air power
roles, that of tactical strike support/interdiction evolved
from the carnage of the First World War. At the
beginning of that conflict, when aircraft were generally
unarmed, it was not unknown for pilots on both sides to
follow Piazza's lead and drop darts, grenades or small
bombs on to the ground forces they were observing.
This could be especially effective against massed troop
formations (particularly if they included horsed transport or cavalry which was susceptible to animal panic)
but was usually regarded as little more than an irritant
through its lack of repetition. But things changed once
the trench system became established. Not only were
the armies situated in one place, which tended to increase their dependence upon static supply dumps and
communications networks behind the front line, but
their artillery came up against problems.

Gunners could not see their targets – vulnerable
though such targets were – and could not observe the
fall of shot. Observation aircraft and balloons could
help to a certain extent, but to be effective the artillery
bombardments needed to be both powerful and sustained. Preliminary barrages lasting days rather than
hours became the norm by 1916, and although these
could be effective, they were extremely expensive and
eroded the element of surprise. In such circumstances
the aircraft was an obvious alternative. Armed with
bombs and machine-guns, it could appear over the
enemy lines, attack the relevant targets and be gone
before the ground forces had fully realized what was
going on. If enough aircraft were used, the task of the
artillery could be done literally in minutes, enabling the
ground forces to advance against a surprised and confused enemy.

The Germans seem to have understood this first: in
late summer 1917, General von Hutier was given the
task of attacking and taking the town of Riga on the
Eastern Front, so that the German armies could
advance along the Baltic coast and turn the right flank
of the Russian line. According to normal practice,
Hutier should have planned a sustained artillery
bombardment before sending his troops forward in a
frontal assault, but rather than risk a repetition of the
many defeats which had followed such tactics in the
past, he chose instead to use aircraft to attack the
Russian lines just ahead of his main force. He did not
dispense with artillery altogether – in fact, his plan
involved a five-hour bombardment, using a mixture of
gas and high explosive – but as the enemy clearly
expected a barrage which would go on for anything up
to four days they would still have their heads down as
the advance got under way. The tactic was a success,
and was repeated on a number of occasions by both
sides as the war progressed. Two months after the Riga
offensive, the British used aircraft to support the newly
invented tanks in their first major battle at Cambrai,
hitting troop concentrations and other targets just in
front of the advancing ground forces, and during the
major German offensive on the Western Front in
March and April 1918, Field Marshal von Hindenburg
used Hutier's tactics to good effect. The groundwork
had been well and truly laid.

If the First World War had continued for a few more
months, into the spring of 1919, there is much to
suggest that the principle of tactical strike support/
interdiction would have been extended still further.
When Colonel J. F. C. Fuller, a staff officer with the
British Tank Corps, observed the confusion which
accompanied the Allied retreat in spring 1918, he was
struck by the ease with which such an organizational
break-down could be achieved and by the advantages
which were likely to accrue to the attacking side. Concentrating for obvious reasons upon the use of the tank,

he compiled a document known originally as "The Tactics of the Attack as affected by the Speed and Circuit of the Medium D Tank" but later shortened to "Plan 1919". As Fuller's tanks advanced in pincer movements on the selected ninety miles of front, air support was to be provided. According to the plan, elements of the newly-constituted Royal Air Force were to indulge in ground strafing just in advance of the armour to help punch the initial holes in the enemy line, while other aircraft bombed important targets in the rear. Chief among these was to be the sector GHQ, the aim being to destroy the "brain" of the enemy rather than his expendable "muscles" or front-line units.

The war ended before Fuller had a chance to test his ideas in action and, as with strategic bombing, a seemingly viable air power theory was left in limbo, unsupported by essential evidence. But in this case the future was not left solely to the theorists, for although cooperation between the army and a proudly-independent Royal Air Force in Britain was poor, other European states were quick to realize the potential. In Russia, for example, once the chaos of the Revolution and Civil War had died down, tactical strike support of ground forces was regarded as essential, and for much of the inter-war period research and development on the air side concentrated upon this role. Consequently, by the late 1930s and early 1940s, the Soviet Air Force consisted almost entirely of tactical strike aircraft, tied closely to the needs of ground forces, and throughout the Russo-German War (1941–1945) such machines as the Petlyakov PE2 and Ilyushin IL2 provided constant support to land units, acting as protection against enemy attack and as forward strike elements.

It was in Germany that the process was carried to its logical conclusion, however, when generals such as

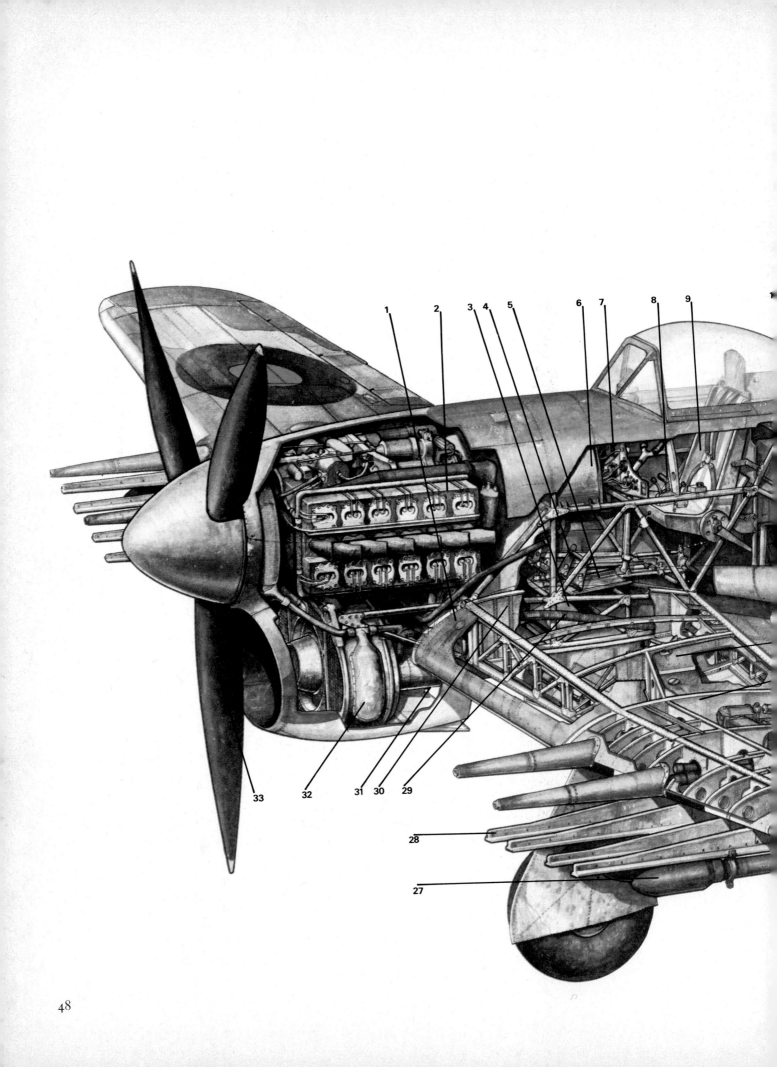

1
2
3 4 5
6 7
8
9

33
32
31 30 29

28

27

48

While the battle of Britain was in progress, with the superlative Supermarine Spitfire and Hawker Hurricane carving their names on the scroll of aviation history, another RAF fighter was being test-flown in great secrecy. This was a basic, no-frills single-seat fighter. But it had one distinction, in the shape of a huge power-plant that, while giving an incredible extra 100mph over the Hurricane, created real and unpleasant problems for the test-pilots who had to fly the prototypes.

1	Leading-edge fuel tank	20	Inner wing-stiffening rib
2	Napier Sabre II engine	21	Intermediate wing-stiffening rib
3	Hydraulic reservoir		
4	Rudder pedals	22	Rear mounting
5	Heel boards	23	Outer wing-stiffening rib
6	Oil tank		
7	Instrument panel	24	Mk 1 Hispano 20mm cannon (four)
8	Throttle control		
9	Pilot's seat	25	Ammunition box
10	Oxygen bottle	26	Flap jack
11	Elevator mass-balance	27	60lb UP HE rockets (four on each wing)
12	Rudder frame		
13	Retractable tail-wheel	28	Rocket rails
14	Elevator control	29	Gun-bay heating duct
15	Tail joint strap	30	Wing-root rib
16	Control cables	31	Radiator shutter jack
17	Radio equipment	32	Radiator
18	Non-slip walkway	33	Three-blade D.H. propeller
19	Fuel tank		

Manstein and Guderian built up an entire structure of war based closely upon Fuller's ideas. Known as *Blitzkrieg*, it was first tested in Spain during the Civil War (1936–39) and brought to perfection during the campaigns in Poland (1939), France (1940) and Russia (1941). The system of *Blitzkrieg* did not merely consist of sustained tank assaults, gaining momentum as the factor of surprise confused a demoralized enemy but provided for the strike support aircraft – notably the Ju87 dive bomber – which contributed enormously to the remarkable string of German successes. Acting as mobile air artillery, such aircraft hit troop concentrations, communications centres, fuel dumps and even civilian refugees, clearing a way for the tanks to come forward. Their screeching sirens and apparent ruthlessness undermined the morale of opposing troops, especially in the French campaign. When the German land forces approached the city of Rotterdam in May 1940, for example, it took only one air raid by medium bombers for the garrison to surrender, and although there is evidence that the strike was unnecessary, its existence discouraged many other cities from even trying to hold out in the future. The lesson which emerged, still bearing considerable relevance today, was that very close cooperation between air and ground elements was an essential pre-requisite to success in modern war.

The importance of this lesson is re-inforced when Allied attempts at tactical strike support during the Second World War are examined. In the French campaign of 1940, for example, aircraft capable of carrying out the role were available, but they were largely of obsolete design while their pilots lacked training in low-level precision attacks or close cooperation with ground forces. This was partly a result of economic stringency during the inter-war years, especially in Britain, but more importantly was a by-product of the emphasis upon strategic bombing and Royal Air Force independence. Resources, both financial and human, had been devoted to the offensive capabilities of the manned bomber fleet, and although something of a *volte-face* had taken place when air defence was suddenly seen as important during the late 1930s, fighters had been preferred to strike aircraft. The abortive attempts to destroy bridges over the Meuse river and Albert Canal in order to stem the German advance in May 1940 show the inevitable outcome: unescorted Fairey Battle light bombers – slow, under-gunned and vulnerable – made little impact for very high losses. Some attempts were made to switch medium bombers such as Bristol Blenheims or Wellingtons to the tactical role, but with little success as their crews had even less experience or expertise. In addition, lacking air supremacy in the face of a large and well-organized Luftwaffe, the Allied aircraft came up against the problem of integrated air defence systems and interceptor fighters. It soon became apparent that the First World War experiments with tactical strike support – restricted as they were to a fairly static battlefield which could be covered quickly by attacking aircraft – had failed to emphasize the crucial point that the enemy may well be capable of preventing you from reaching the target, let alone destroying it.

Regardless of these basic lessons, however tactical strike support interdiction does not seem to have been afforded the priority it deserved by the Allied powers, until about 1944. During the British campaigns in North Africa (1940–43) for example, there was still a lack of specially developed machines, and for much of the time both bombers and fighters were switched to the tactical strike role as and when they were needed. Aircraft such as the Blenheim (designed for strategic bombing and incapable of attaining the speed necessary for successful tactical strike) and the Spitfire and Hurricane (interceptor fighters which, although enjoying the speed, lacked the payload capability were ill-suited. Attempts were made to rectify the situation in preparation for the D-Day invasion but were left too late. An entire air force, the 2nd Tactical, was formed, with bombers like the American Marauder being used for tactical bombing and interdiction, and the British

A Junkers Ju-87, known to Allies and Axis forces as the Stuka an acronym for Dive Bomber, starts the roll that precedes its dive on to the target. Dive bombing allowed bombers to hit small targets very accurately, and enabled the Germans to destroy transport, command centres and even gun positions prior to a land assault — it was a vital part of their Blitzkrieg tactics.

Typhoon for close support of ground forces. When the Allied High Command at last realized the desperate need for tactical strike support interdiction over the coastal areas of North-West Europe in 1944, they had to order a large-scale switch of strategic bombers away from the attacks upon Germany.

The results were impressive, but ill-considered. The invasion began with wide-ranging attacks along the length of the coast of northern France to confuse the enemy, with an ultimate aim of cutting off the entire area behind the proposed landing sites in Normandy, between the rivers Orne and Vire. The strategic bombers did their job well, destroying bridges, railroads, roads, communications centres and possible defensive systems but, if anything, went too far. Not only were the Germans paralyzed, and unable to move reinforcements into the battle area but, when the Allies emerged from the beach-heads in August 1944, they, too, found it difficult to advance. The bombers were too powerful, for instead of blasting a route for the ground forces, as the Stukas had done in the *blitzkrieg* operations, they had presented the advancing armies with a sea of rubble, much of which was impassable.

Take, for example, the case of Caen, a city which should have been taken on D-Day itself. When it proved a centre of resistance, the bombers attacked it with such force that no wheeled or tracked vehicle could pass through it, thus necessitating by-pass operations (*Epsom* and *Goodwood*) which were both lengthy and costly. In addition, instead of destroying defending forces, the bombing had presented the Germans with almost impregnable positions, which required bitter

house-to-house fighting before the Allies were successful. A similar situation had arisen during the battle for Monte Cassino in Italy during March 1944, when over 1000 tons of bombs had not only destroyed an historic monastery but also provided the Germans with good defensive positions.

In fairness, however, it should be added that improvements were made as the war drew to an end, with the specially designed light or medium bombers and fighter bombers, especially of the 2nd Tactical Air Force, learning to cooperate with the ground forces. Indeed, by late 1944, during the abortive German offensive in the Ardennes, the appearance of tactical strike aircraft over the American lines, after a period of bad weather had prevented them taking off, effectively turned the tide of the battle. Similarly, in the American "island-hopping" campaigns in the Pacific (1943–45), U.S. Marine Corps fighter-bombers perfected ground attack techniques with bombs, rockets, and napalm. By 1945, after a long and often difficult process of error and experimentation, the Allies seem to have appreciated the role of tactical strike support interdiction, but it is probably more than mere coincidence that much of their success occurred only after air supremacy had been gained by other means, notably the American strategic attacks against the Luftwaffe and its supporting services. In the absence of opposing fighters, experiments could be made in ground attack techniques.

Once the Second World War was over, the importance of tactical strike support/interdiction was overshadowed by the apparent success of strategic bombing using atomic weapons. The future seemed to be sure to involve atomic exchanges, leaving little room for conventional warfare. But this did not last. Once the Soviets had exploded their first atomic device in 1949, and the principle of mutual deterrence between the super powers began to emerge, the possibility of fighting non-nuclear limited wars for limited political aims soon became apparent, re-introducing all the old techniques of conventional conflict. This can be seen clearly in the Korean War (1950–53) when the Americans, in company with the United Nations, limited the size of committed forces, the scope of the geographical area of conflict and the political aims and types of weapons used in what was, to all intents and purposes, a peripheral theatre of East-West hostility. The limitation of weapons inevitably restricted the air element considerably, for although the American air force had the capability to launch strategic bombing raids on

Ground attack in theory and practice. A Hurricane IID starts its run firing armour piercing ammunition against an enemy tank. Below: A Typhoon equipped to carry bombs. Far right: How a rocket firing fighter would attack a target like a railway train. The pilot had to align his aircraft with the target and then fire the rocket when he was within range before peeling off.

North Korea and the Chinese bases across the Yalu river with either conventional or nuclear weapons, a political desire to keep both the Chinese and the Russians out of the war, necessitated a return to tactical air attacks. So far as ground forces were concerned, this resulted in little more than an extension of World War II techniques to a new theatre of operation, with fighter bombers giving close support and taking out enemy strong-points immediately in advance of the front line. But the process of interdiction reached new levels of application. Confronted by an enemy who received supplies and, after late 1950, reinforcements, over a lengthy border with Communist China, the Americans attempted to cut off North Korea by destroying the bridges, roads, tracks and supply-routes which connected the two countries. On the whole, the campaign was fairly successful, even when it was insisted that not one bomb should fall on Chinese territory for fear of political repercussions.

The situation in Vietnam in the mid 1960s was very similar and, as we have seen, the Americans tried to repeat the Korean offensive by instigating a campaign of tactical interdiction designed to cut off the North from all contact with the South. The North Vietnamese government was openly supporting the Viet Cong guerrillas south of the 17th Parallel, pushing both supplies and reinforcements across the Demilitarized Zone and down what was known as the Ho Chi Minh Trail, a long and tortuous route which wound its way through the neighbouring countries of Laos and Cambodia before emerging in the Mekong Delta around Saigon. Air strikes against these areas began in 1965, but the success enjoyed in Korea was not repeated. There were a number of reasons for this which, when combined together, showed how difficult the role of tactical strike support/interdiction had become.

The common denominator undoubtedly lay in the technological revolution which took place during the 1960s. On the air side, the trend was toward the multi-role aircraft, capable of carrying out a number of tasks where speed was essential – for example, reconnaissance or interception – and this tended to act against the tactical strike potential. As early as the Second World War, the accuracy of strikes had been dubious and it had become apparent that the faster an aircraft travelled, the less likely it was to hit a precise target which remained in the pilot's sight for a very short time. As aircraft became virtually supersonic, therefore, the chances of hitting a camouflaged supply dump or a

narrow trail in the jungle declined, leaving only two options open to the attacking side. The Americans tried both in Vietnam between 1965 and 1973. To begin with they attempted to substitute firepower for accuracy, dropping increasingly larger loads of high explosive and napalm on to the smaller targets in the hopes of hitting them with something. But this was expensive and, in the event, less than successful as the Viet Cong showed themselves to be remarkably adept at improvisation and recovery. The alternative was improved technology, particularly in the areas of directing bombs and radio controlled guidance; a process which began with the introduction of laser and TV-guided "smart" bombs and culminated in the development of tactical strike RPVs, armed with missiles, bombs and computer control systems. The results were promising, for in 1972 and early 1973 a number of strikes upon the infiltration areas appear to have succeeded, and many would argue that their introduction contributed to the North Vietnamese decision for a truce with the Americans.

Nevertheless, this is only half the picture, for although the Americans may have solved the problems of accurate delivery, they were also presented with enormous difficulties by anti-aircraft defences which destroyed a significant number of tactical aircraft. The development of air defence systems will be examined in more depth in a later chapter, but it is necessary to stress that as the role of tactical strike

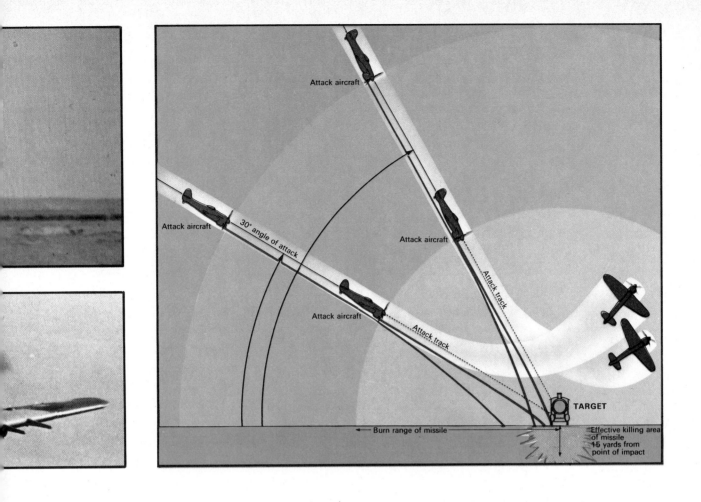

Attack aircraft

Attack aircraft

30° angle of attack

Attack aircraft

Attack aircraft

Attack aircraft

Attack track

Attack track

TARGET

Burn range of missile

Effective killing area of missile 15 yards from point of impact

support/interdiction evolved, so did the enemy's capability to destroy attacking aircraft. During the Second World War – and in Korea as well – interceptor fighters had been the main problem, but by the time of Vietnam ground-based units had increased in effectiveness and importance. Chief among these were the SAMs (Surface-to-Air Missiles), capable of homing-in on the exhaust heat of a jet-engined aircraft, and although the North Vietnamese and Viet Cong forces had access to only the first generation of these weapons – the Soviet-built SAMs 2, 3 and manportable 7 – they proved effective in destroying the American Phantoms and Skyhawks. By the early 1970s they also had Soviet self-propelled anti-aircraft cannon such as the radar-controlled ZSU-23/4 as well as conventional A.A. guns, so it may be appreciated that the Americans were encountering stiff opposition. They tried to counter the SAMs by re-introducing piston-driven aircraft and depending upon helicopter gun ships (a process which incidentally aided accuracy by reducing the speed of attack), and attempted to jam the ZSUs radar through ECM, but overall the problem remained. It is still applicable today, as the NATO air forces are well aware, for in the event of war with the Warsaw Pact Countries in Central Europe any attempts at tactical strike support/interdiction – against bridges, airfields and advancing enemy forces – are sure to be vigorously opposed. Technology appears to have caused a continuous battle between offensive and defensive capa-

bilities, and it is nowhere more apparent than in this particular role.

It would be wrong, however, to suppose that tactical strike support/interdiction is a declining air power task: far from it. The basic principles behind its original development still remain: for if an army is to operate successfully in any situation, it needs to attack the enemy in every possible way and, regardless of the problems, the aircraft still offers an unprecedented degree of mobility, speed and hitting power which military weapons short of tactical nuclear strength cannot hope to emulate. In addition, the technological developments continue apace and may in fact outweigh the defensive capabilities of the enemy ground or air forces. For tactical strike the Americans now have fleets of helicopters, designed to hug the ground before appearing suddenly to attack advancing enemy forces: the British have the Hawker Harrier "jump jet" which can land and take off vertically from extremely small areas, thus enabling it to survive counter-strikes and return to the attack with surprise on its side. At the same time, for the interdiction role, the ALCM, with conventional warhead, now has the ability to attack the most inaccessible and well-defended target through its contour-matching guidance system with an impressive degree of accuracy. Such developments suggest a technological swing in favour of the offensive, at least for the moment, and explain the importance placed upon the continued use of tactical strike/interdiction.

Transport and Airborne Landings

Dakotas stream across the sky as 9000 paratroops jump over Le Muy in southern France. The airborne attack supporting the Anvil sea landings in 1944 was one of the most successful attacks of its kind in history.

The third air-power role to be examined in a tactical context is that of transport/airborne landings. It inevitably covers a large amount of ground, but the two concepts involved are inextricably linked not only by the idea of movement through the air, but also by the very similar types of aircraft which tend to be used for both sorts of operation. Having said that, however, it is perhaps easier to take the two topics separately to a certain extent, if only because before 1940 airborne landings as such had never been practised under war conditions.

Air transport can be taken to cover the movement of conventional ground forces (as opposed to specially trained paratroop units), equipment and supplies from one place to another through the air. This has obvious advantages in both the planning and execution of military campaigns. If ground troops find themselves cut off from the main army by an advancing enemy, or are operating behind enemy lines as part of a definite strategy, or if the ground being fought over is unsuitable, aircraft can help solve the problems. They can be used to keep troops supplied, either by para-dropping material to them or, if an airfield is available, by landing to evacuate civilians, casualties or unnecessary administrative troops, while at the same time reinforcing existing combat units. Similarly, if the enemy attacks a weak portion of the front line or a poorly defended locality far from base, men and material can be packed into aircraft and flown to the trouble spot quickly. Aircraft give a new and significant amount of mobility and flexibility to the ground forces.

There is evidence to suggest that these capabilities were recognized as early as the First World War. In the campaign against the Turks in Mesopotamia, for example, when British troops were besieged in the fortress of Kut-el-Amara between December 1915 and their surrender in April 1916, the Royal Flying Corps attempted supply drops to the starving garrison. Their efforts were crude by modern standards, entailing a low-level swoop over the fortress so that the observer could push sacks of food, medical supplies and other essential material over the side of the aircraft. The methods were a little short on success as no one had yet thought of attaching parachutes to break the fall. Many supplies were destroyed on impact, but at least the basic idea was there: it was to be remembered and built upon during the inter-war period.

The other element of air transport – the movement of troops to battle areas – was not attempted during the First World War, but experiments began quite soon after the end of that conflict. During the early 1920s, in an effort to preserve the independence of the Royal Air Force by making it as indispensable as possible, Trenchard and the air chiefs managed to station squadrons in the main trouble spots of the Empire to aid the ground forces in keeping the peace. At first this consisted of bombing isolated villages belonging to recalcitrant tribes in places like Iraq or the northern frontiers of India – areas inaccessible to the military without lengthy forced marches – but by about 1923 the idea of actually flying troops out to trouble spots seems to have occurred. Standards of comfort must have been abysmal in aircraft designed for other tasks, but the precedent was established. It was reinforced in December 1928 when the Royal Air Force successfully evacuated 586 British civilians from Kabul in Afghanistan, then in the throes of a bitter civil war, and thereafter the idea became widely accepted.

As with most air power roles, the opportunity to develop these ideas along the lines already laid down came with the Second World War. For geographical reasons, most examples that could be cited tended to be in difficult areas, where normal ground or sea movement was curtailed by problems of distance or physical barriers, and in this context the Allied campaigns in Burma and southern China between 1942 and 1945 perhaps offer the best illustrations. After the British forces had retreated through Burma to the Indian border in 1942, the problem of supply was immense. With the loss of Rangoon, all war material and reinforcements had to be brought to the front line from Calcutta and central India – a journey which could take up to two months overland – and the supply route to Chiang Kai-shek's Nationalist Chinese forces had been cut entirely by the advancing Japanese. If the British were to be sustained on the Imphal plain and the Chinese (dependent as they were for most of their arms and military equipment upon the Americans) kept in the war at all, some alternative method of supply was desperately needed. It was provided by aircraft.

Between late 1942 and early 1945 American and British pilots, flying C-47 Dakota transports, completed endless supply missions from India "over the hump" of the Himalayan foothills to southern China, bolstering the efforts of Chiang Kai-shek and, between June and November 1944, sustaining the B-29 strategic bombers in their campaign against the Japanese homeland. At the same time the British forces around Imphal and

Kohima were re-inforced and re-equipped; a process which reached new heights of urgency in early 1944 when the Japanese, in one of their last land offensives, laid siege to both localities. Indeed, as the sieges began to take effect, the entire 5th Indian Infantry Division, complete with its mules and essential fighting equipment, was air-lifted from Arakan on the eastern coast of Burma into Imphal itself; a feat which, at the time, constituted the largest air-movement of combat troops ever attempted. The arrival of these troops at Imphal is regarded by many as the turning point of the battle. Furthermore, while all this was going on, Brigadier Orde Wingate's Chindit patrols were operating behind Japanese lines, having been lifted in by air and depending solely upon re-supply by Dakotas for their survival.

This does not mean, of course, that all air movement and transport was successful. German efforts to supply the beleaguered garrison of Stalingrad on the Eastern Front in late 1942, for example, failed because of a shortage of suitable aircraft and a spirited defence of air space by Russian fighters, while similar efforts by the Royal Air Force over Arnhem in September 1944 made little difference to an already desperate situation. The lessons to be drawn would appear to be two-fold. Firstly, transport aircraft tend, almost by definition, to be slow moving and so require protection from both air interception and ground defences – considerations which imply that they can be used successfully only if you enjoy air superiority, at least on a local level – and that a substantial fleet of transports is essential if large numbers of troops are to be moved or supplied. If these

two prerequisites are satisfied, air transport will probably work; if one or both are unobtainable, it will more than likely fail.

Post-war examples re-inforce this theory. In late 1953, when the French were fighting desperately against the Viet Minh guerillas in northern Indo-China (now Vietnam), they established an isolated fortified base at Dien Bien Phu in an effort to draw the enemy, under General Giap, away from northern Laos. For a time all appeared to go well, with the French parachutists receiving regular supplies and reinforcements by air, using an airstrip carved out of the valley floor but, at this stage, opposition was slight. Then, in March 1954, the Viet Minh attacked, having approached Dien Bien Phu secretly. They managed to take the surrounding hills, unfortified by the French who thought that air superiority would make the fortress impregnable, and even brought up anti-aircraft guns from the Chinese border. Once these were established Dien Bien Phu was cut off, aircraft could not use an air-strip overlooked from all sides and ground forces could not approach the fortress through miles of dense and hostile jungle. The siege lasted fifty-six days, during which the French made repeated efforts to keep the garrison supplied by air-drops, but with a shortage of aircraft and the heavy Viet Minh anti-air defence, smaller and smaller amounts of essential equipment got through. In the end, supply drops became harder to deliver accurately to the striking perimeter and the garrison was forced to surrender. As had been the case at Stalingrad twelve years before, air transport had

An American McDonnell Douglas YC-15 jet transport makes a low pass during a flight demonstration. The YC-15 is capable of carrying 150 fully-equipped men or 62,000lb of equipment.

failed because of a shortage of aircraft and a successful defence of air space by a determined enemy.

At the other end of the scale, however, successes still occur. During the Arab-Israeli War of October 1973, for example, both the Americans and Russians, in possession of large transport fleets and acting with freedom from ground or air opposition, were able to deliver vast quantities of supplies into the war zone for the Israelis and Arabs. Air transport is therefore still a viable proposition if the conditions are right, and the fact that NATO strategy in the event of a Warsaw Pact attack depends to a certain extent upon the movement of reserves by air from America and Britain to the Central Front or flanks would imply that many expect those conditions to be easily found. How viable this is remains to be seen, for the recent decision to phase out the Royal Air Force Transport Command must undermine one of its basic foundations. However, this cannot alter the fact that the aircraft has given to the supply and movement processes a unique degree of flexibility and mobility.

The same general conclusion applies to airborne landings, for although they have had a shorter history, their impact upon the tactics of war has been considerable. The reasons are fairly obvious. If you are on the offensive and able to put in a powerful assault behind the enemy lines, this will clearly have an unsettling – even demoralizing – effect. Whatever the target for such an assault, the enemy will be forced to look two ways at once, withdrawing units from his front line or committing important reserves to deal with the new situation, and this will inevitably weaken his capacity to withstand the main frontal attack. If, in addition, you have directed the airborne assault against specific tactical strong-points or positions, the main attack will be further aided by the destruction of fortresses, airfields or concentration areas or by the taking and holding of bridges or road systems. Even on the defensive, there are advantages. An airborne landing behind the advancing enemy columns can disrupt their supply lines and communications, while weakening their strength as elements are forced to move back to counter the unexpected attack. In such cases there is, of course, little chance of the airborne troops being relieved as the main force will probably be retreating away from them, but the idea has been put into practice sufficiently often, particularly by the French in Indo-China (1946–54), to merit some consideration.

Airborne landings as such were not put into effect

until 1940, but in the years before a number of experiments had been effected which prepared the way. As early as 1918 the theorist Billy Mitchell, convinced to the point of extremism that air power could achieve victory, suggested training the 1st American Infantry Division in the art of parachuting and then dropping them from converted Handley-Page 1500s behind the enemy line to capture the city of Metz. The war ended before he could convince anyone in high command that his scheme was even worth contemplating, and it was not until 1927 that military parachuting was attempted. In that year eight Italian soldiers jumped as a team in full battle kit, and this may be regarded as the first successful human airdrop for purely military purposes. The Italians did not take their experiments very much further, however, leaving the large-scale development to Russia and Germany for the rest of the inter-war period. Initially, during the late 1920s and early 1930s, these two countries followed basically similar lines, chiefly because German soldiers and airmen, restricted by the terms of the Versailles Treaty to a very passive military role, conducted clandestine training in Russia. The experiments seem to have concentrated upon parachuting, for by the mid 1930s both countries possessed substantial airborne arms. The Germans had to wait until their invasion of Austria in 1938 before displaying their capability *en masse*, but the Russians were impressing foreign observers with parachute displays as early as the military manoeuvre of 1936 when, in a mock battle around Moscow, a total of 5200 fully-armed men descended from the skies. Meanwhile the

Germans had added another aspect to airborne landings through their experiments with gliders, begun as a secret method of training conventional pilots in the basic elements of flying. By the mid 1930s this was recognized as an important means of dispatching troops and equipment into battle behind the enemy lines.

With such equipment and experience available, it is little wonder that the Germans laid great stress upon their airborne potential as soon as the Second World War began. Their first – and many would argue, most successful – operation took place in May 1940, during the invasion of France and the Low Countries. When planning the overall campaign the Germans had originally thought along the lines of a repetition of 1914 – the strong right hook through the Low Countries aimed at Paris – but after a copy of the written orders had inadvertently fallen into Allied hands, the *blitzkrieg* practitioners, led by von Manstein, managed to persuade Hitler to permit an armoured thrust through the relatively undefended Ardennes region. This pre-supposed that the Allies would have advanced into Belgium to protect that area, so leaving the route to the Channel coast open, and for this reason an attack had still to be made upon the Low Countries to force such a commitment and to act as the northern part of a vast "nutcracker" operation. Field Marshal von Bock's Army Group "B" was detailed for this northern attack, with the Belgian fortress of Eben Emael, covering the approaches to the Meuse river and Albert Canal just south of Maastricht, as a primary objective. Designed to withstand all the most likely conventional attacks, the

A German Messerschmitt Gigant, Giant, the biggest operational transport aircraft of the war. The Gigant was slow and unwieldy and was effective only as long as the Germans had air superiority.

fortress was a potentially dangerous block, not only to von Bock's advance but also to the Ardennes assault which needed flank protection. A frontal attack would be extremely costly and would certainly fail but the new found flexibility and surprise of an airborne landing seemed to offer a solution. So before daylight on May 10 1940, a glider borne force of specially trained sappers landed on top of the fortress and began a systematic destruction of casements and turrets. At the same time, other small glider detachments seized bridges over the Albert Canal and one over the river at Maastricht. On May 11 the Belgian garrison of Eben Emael – over 1000 strong – surrendered. The airborne troops were relieved by ground units within twenty-four hours, before the Allies could react, and von Bock's forces advanced against little opposition. The potential of airborne landings was fully established.

Not all airborne assaults have been this successful, for the practical problems are immense. In the first place it is unrealistic to expect major victories from air-landed troops – on their own they are just not strong enough to decide a campaign. Because of their dependence upon aircraft they are not heavily armed, lacking both armour and heavy artillery, while the restrictions of re-supply mean that they can hold out for little more than forty-eight hours. Add to these factors the problems of weather, terrain, communications and target selection, and it is obvious that the planning and execution of airborne landings is a delicate business, becoming progressively more delicate the larger the landing to be effected. Both the Axis and

Allied powers discovered this to their cost during the Second World War.

In the case of the German attack upon Crete in May 1941, it was far too ambitious to be completely success-ful. The airborne troops were to take the entire island virtually on their own, and were then to use it as a stepping-stone for further attack upon Cyprus and even Alexandria. General Student, the German airborne commander, had nearly 23,000 men at his disposal – the bulk of Germany's airborne potential – but a lack of JU-52 transport aircraft in which to carry them. A proportion could be taken by glider, and a small number by sea, but if concentration of force was to be achieved, at least one of the three airfields on the island at Maleme, Retimo and Hearaklion had to be taken to allow men to be landed in conventional aircraft. Even then, the initial assault force of 10,000 parachutists had to be divided into three waves as the JU-52s in Greece could only lift a third of the force at any one time. The result was a dangerous diversification of effort, with very costly attacks at different times against each of the airfields. It was only the demoralized state of the Allied garrison that led to eventual German success. After ten days of fighting (May 20-30 1941) the British retreated to the south of the island and were evacuated to North Africa, but the cost to the airborne forces was enormous.

One in four of the German parachutists had been killed, entire battalions had been wiped out; JU-52s had been shot down in alarming numbers and any thought of further assaults in the area had to be discarded. It was a Pyrrhic victory, sounding the death-knell of a German airborne force which had been asked to do too much.

Almost exactly the same happened to the British 1st Airborne Division at Arnhem in September 1944. Their assault on the Dutch town was part of an elaborate airborne plan – code-named Operation *Market Garden* – in which a series of vital bridges at Eindhoven, Veghel, Grave, Nijmegen and Arnhem would be taken and held while the British Second and U.S. First Armies advanced in a rapier-like thrust for northern Holland and, from there, the industrial heartland of Germany. On paper the plan was ambitious but the potential gains were immense, for without the bridges the waterways of Holland could hold up the advance for weeks. In the event, the bulk of the operation was a success, with the British Guards Armoured Division punching through on the ground to link up with the U.S. 101st and 82nd Airborne Divisions at Eindhoven and Nijmegen respectively, but the forces at Arnhem were just too far away. In addition, the 1st Airborne had been dropped too far away from the objective and, although a small group did take and hold the bridge for a short time against tremendous odds, the rest of the force was trapped in fierce fighting which made any attempt at breakout towards the relieving forces impossible to coordinate. It also complicated the process of re-supply as there was no one drop-zone which could serve the whole division, and even when a Polish parachute brigade was put in as reinforcement, the problems remained. They were not eased by the unexpected vehemence of German opposition – the 9th and 10th SS Panzer Divisions had unfortunately chosen the Arnhem area in which to refit after the D-Day battles and so were on hand to counter the element of surprise – nor by a general lack of good communications due to faulty wireless equipment. After nine days of bitter fighting, the 1st Airborne was ordered to withdraw. Of approximately 9000 men dropped since September 17, only about 2400 made their way out on the 25th: once again the airborne units had been asked to do too much.

These two examples should not, of course, be taken to prove that airborne landings during World War II were dogged by failure: on the contrary, there were many successful operations, such as the invasion of Sicily in July 1943, the Normandy landings of June 1944 and the crossing of the Rhine in March 1945, but in all these cases the airborne troops were only expected to take specific tactical objectives which would be consolidated and held by rapidly advancing ground forces. The lesson seems to be that the smaller the committed force and, more important, the less ambitious the objectives, the greater the chance of success. Airborne landings are in essence limited tactical operations; to expect more is to expect too much.

Looking at the situation since 1945, this lesson seems to have been absorbed by those countries that can still afford the luxury of an airborne capability with all its attendant specialist training and equipment. With the possible exception of Dien Bien Phu in 1953/4, most post-war airborne assaults have been tactical affairs, opening the way in fairly unambitious terms for a ground or seaborne attack. The Anglo-French expedition to Suez in November 1956, for example, envisaged parachute drops which were merely a prelude to a seaborne invasion, and although super power pressure forced an end to the operation before it had been completed, this general pattern of events was certainly being followed. Similarly in July 1974 the Turks used their airborne forces to take the high ground in the Kyrenia Mountains of Cyprus which overlooked their landing beaches, and then relieved them quickly before advancing towards Nicosia. Small operations therefore seem to be the key to success, and the trend today in many countries, at least in the West, is to cut down the size of specially trained, expensive airborne units, replacing them with heli-borne forces which seem to offer a new potential, particularly in the difficult area of counter-insurgency. After all, helicopters are relatively cheap, the troops which use them do not need to be trained in completely new skills, and operations involving them can achieve the important element of surprise which slow-moving transport aircraft cannot match. In addition, they are not so dependent upon air superiority, being able to fly below radar cover and at speeds which make their destruction by ground units significantly more difficult. Two examples from the 1973 Arab-Israeli War illustrate the point: on October 6 a Syrian heli-borne force was able to take the important Israeli fortress on top of Mount Hermon with relative ease. On the Israeli side, as the war progressed and the new SAMs and ZSUs threatened to destroy escorting fighters or ground-

attack aircraft, it was reported that Israeli parachute troops refused to jump from slow-moving vulnerable transport aircraft. Technology seems to have destroyed many of the advantages associated with the parachute and glider, although it is interesting to note that the Warsaw Pact still maintains seven regular airborne divisions, with full reserve backing. Clearly, if you can afford to maintain such troops, are virtually guaranteed of air superiority and are planning a swift offensive to link up with troops dropped behind the enemy lines, the airborne potential may still be a viable proposition. Such circumstances are now so rare, however, that few countries really contemplate their regular occurance.

It might be tempting to conclude (reviewing the tactics covered so far) that the aircraft has contributed almost solely to the support of forces on land. This impression is false, however, for, although the processes of transportation, airborne landings and, to a certain extent, strike support are inextricably linked to land operations, the impact of the aircraft has been just as dramatic so far as naval warfare is concerned.

When the war potential of aircraft was first recognized just before the First World War, naval leaders were, if anything, more enthusiastic than their military counterparts. In Britain, for example, the Admiralty encouraged naval officers to learn the new art of flying, and when the Royal Flying Corps (RFC) was formed as a part of the Royal Engineers in May 1912 it included a Naval Wing, initially designed to provide the Navy with the same sort of basic reconnaissance that the Military Wing would give to the Army. The Royal Engineers were a military formation under the control of the War

Office and the inter-service cooperation implied by the inclusion of naval personnel within its ranks could not be expected to last. As a result, by 1914, a separate Royal Naval Air Service (RNAS) had come into existence under Admiralty control. Its duties were unclear, and for a time it merely duplicated the evolving roles of the RFC, but as the First World War progressed it acted as a centre for experimentation and new ideas. When Zeppelin airships attacked naval installations in England as early as 1914, for example, it was RNAS aircraft which were first used in a bombing counter-offensive, hitting Zeppelin sheds as far afield as Cologne and Dusseldorf before the war was six months old. Similarly in 1915, they were the first to be used in air defence when the Navy was given responsibility for trying to shoot down the airships as they raided English towns.

But these were roles which could be – and were – taken over by the other services, and it was not until 1917 that purely naval needs were identified and met. In an age when the fleet was the most important manifestation of naval power, the advantages of aircraft at sea with the capital ships, warning of enemy vessels approaching and tracking submarines, were quickly appreciated. At first, of course, continuous air cover was restricted to areas of sea within range of land, as the aircraft were dependent upon their airfields, and even when experiments were extended to the idea of seaplanes, the necessity of calm water conditions for take-off and landing precluded their presence in many of the important naval areas. But in 1917 the idea of mobile, sea-going air bases was successfully tried,

when a Sopwith Camel fighter of the RNAS took off from and landed upon H.M.S. *Argus*, a converted merchant ship. The aircraft carrier had been born, although it was not to be tried in action before the end of the First World War.

Unlike many other aspects of air power, however, this particular innovation was not ignored during the inter-war period, and although there was no evidence to support the efficacy of the aircraft carrier in a war situation, the major naval powers could not afford to do without it. Consequently, in a period when genuine efforts were being made to limit the size of world navies, with countries scrapping perfectly usable vessels as late as the 1930s, a minor arms race took place, principally among America, Britain and Japan, in the building of aircraft carriers. The reasons are understandable, for all three powers were concerned, or aimed to be concerned, with spreading or maintaining their influence over wide areas of ocean – Britain through the protection of imperial sea-lanes, America and Japan through their growing rivalry in the Pacific. In such circumstances, the flexibility and mobility of aircraft staying with the fleet at all times offered significant advantages, not least in the protection of the fleet itself. By the late 1930s, all three powers had considerable aircraft-carrier potential, the results of which were to be seen during the Second World War.

This was not the only air-power role to affect the naval side of warfare during the inter-war period. For if aircraft could act as early-warning devices and submarine-trackers, there was no reason why they should not extend their duties to include strike support, destroying enemy vessels before they even came in sight of the main fleet. Mitchell, as we have seen, was an ardent believer in the vulnerability of capital ships to air attack but, despite his graphic illustration of the potential when his aircraft sank the *Ostfriesland* in 1921, few believed the threat to be a real one. Never-

The helicopter in Vietnam. The Americans had vast numbers which were used for liaison, ground attack, troop carrying and evacuating wounded. Helicopters enabled them to penetrate remote jungle areas and reinforce troops under attack by the Viet Cong.

theless, even at this early stage it was possible to define fairly clearly the potentialities of naval aircraft, dividing them basically into offensive and defensive roles. On the offensive, the main advantage was the ability of aircraft to attack and destroy enemy shipping, so weakening his overall strength; on the defensive to search out enemy vessels, warn of their approach and protect the fleet when they, or their attendant aircraft, attacked.

Aircraft contributed significantly in all areas of sea conflict throughout the Second World War. So far as its offensive capabilities were concerned, there is even evidence to suggest that the aircraft changed the course of naval history by assisting in destroying the pre-eminence of the battleship, basically by following the ideas put forward by Mitchell in the early 1920s. As early as November 11 1940, when British Swordfish torpedo bombers from H.M.S. *Illustrious* damaged or destroyed a total of three Italian battleships in Toranto harbour, the vulnerability of capital ships to air attack, doubted by so many before the war began, was effectively proved. Not that this convinced the sceptics entirely. Many naval commanders still dismissed the idea of air attack as little more than an irritant, to be dealt with by anti-aircraft guns which were better organized than those of the Italians, but the evidence gradually piled up against them. In May 1941, for example, it was another Swordfish attack which crippled the German battleship *Bismarck*, slowing her down to the extent that she could be surrounded and destroyed by surface vessels. And seven months later, on 7 December 1941, the surprise attack upon Pearl Harbor

by Japanese aircraft, which destroyed or severely damaged some eight American battleships, should have left no doubts at all. Yet within three days of Pearl Harbor, the British battleship *Prince of Wales*, together with the battle-cruiser *Repulse*, was sunk by Japanese air attack off the eastern coast of Malaya. No naval commander could now venture out to sea, nor indeed remain in harbour, without anxiously scanning the skies for enemy aircraft.

It did not take very long to realize, however, that an effective form of naval protection against air attack was to provide constant air cover for the fleet, and this quite naturally brought the aircraft carrier firmly to the fore. Nowhere was this more apparent than in the massive sea areas of the Pacific, where both contending powers, America and Japan, began the war with large numbers of such vessels. Their existence gave the

major battles of the campaign a unique character, with rival fleets fighting through their aircraft rather than their surface vessels. The aim almost became one of gaining air supremacy, with the main targets invariably the enemy's aircraft carriers. The side which managed to destroy the most aircraft or their support vessels tended to force the other to withdraw and so win the battle. The first intimation of this new style of warfare came in May 1942 in the Battle of the Coral Sea, when each side tried to knock out the other's aircraft carriers by air attack. In the event, both suffered losses and the outcome was uncertain, but the Americans kept a slight advantage by managing to repair the carrier *Lexington* before the Japanese could recover. As a result, in the following month at Midway, American air strength was such that it led to the destruction of four Japanese fleet carriers and forced

Air power at sea, SBD Dauntless dive-bombers on the deck of the USS *Lexington*. They have returned from sinking the Japanese light carrier *Shoho*. A day after this picture was taken the *Lexington* herself fell victim to Japanese carrier-based air attacks.

the enemy to stop its wide-ranging naval actions. From then on Japanese battleships and cruisers had to keep to areas which could be covered by land-based aircraft, leaving the Americans with virtual control of the central Pacific. When the land-based potential was destroyed as well, chiefly at the Battle of the Philippine Sea in June 1944, Japanese naval power was, to all intents and purposes, at an end and American victory was in sight.

An interesting characteristic of the Pacific naval battles, particularly Coral Sea and Midway, was that the actual fleets rarely came into visual contact, sometimes steaming away from each other at distances up to 200 miles apart, leaving the aircraft to do the fighting. In many ways this was indicative of the effect that air power had on naval affairs as a whole, for it was also apparent in the Battle of the Atlantic, even though the aircraft was carrying out its defensive role for much of the time. When the German U-boat campaign, coupled with her surface potential and land-based air capability, threatened to cut the vital British life-line with her Empire, and after the Lend-Lease Act of March 1941, America as well, some form of air cover for the convoys was clearly essential. At first this was provided by long-range Coastal Command aircraft such as the Short Sunderland or land-based Liberator, flying from bases in Northern Ireland, Scotland and even Iceland, but they lacked the range to escort vessels more than about a third of the way across the Atlantic. When America entered the war, she too contributed aircraft from her side of the ocean, but this still left a gap in the centre, within which the convoys, devoid of reconnaissance, submarine early-warning and basic air protection, suffered their most grievous losses. It was not until special escort-carriers, equipped with fighter-bombers, were introduced in 1942 that the "air-gap" was closed. Similar techniques were used in both the Mediterranean and the Pacific, contributing to victories which established the aircraft as an essential defensive as well as offensive aid to naval warfare.

There can be little doubt that these roles remain important, although the post-war period has seen something of a decline in naval air potential. Britain is usually put forward as an example, for naval support has suffered considerably as a result of cuts in defence spending. To a certain extent this is understandable and is probably an inevitable outcome of the withdrawal from imperial commitments. At the same time,

vastly improved aircraft ranges and in-flight refuelling facilities have enabled most sea areas to be adequately patrolled from shore bases alone, and when this is added to the expense factor, the decision to phase out aircraft carriers – the most obvious manifestations of naval air potential – is easily comprehensible. At the moment one such vessel, H.M.S. *Ark Royal*, still remains in Britain, but it is destined for the scrapyard by 1980: a fact which leads many commentators to write off the ability of the British to protect their navy from air attack or to contribute to its strike potential is by no means devoid of its air cover.

This, however, ignores the impact of new techniques, for despite the disappearance of floating airfields which were always highly vulnerable targets, the British Navy

role, the development of Thru'-Deck cruisers, designed to do the jobs of carrier and fighting ship combined, maintain the strike potential of the fleet at sea, particularly when equipped with attack helicopters or VTOL (vertical take-off and landing) aircraft such as the Sea Harrier. For the defensive, long-range reconnaissance aircraft such as the Nimrod can act very effectively as the early warning "eyes" of the fleet, while specially equipped helicopters like the Sea King can track submarines and warn of an enemy approach far more effectively than Second World War carrier-based aircraft. The trend, as elsewhere, is towards multi-role equipment, whereby technology can make possible an increasing flexibility of both aircraft and ships by precluding the need to design them for specific roles.

Admittedly the aircraft carrier is far from dead – in areas such as Vietnam or the Eastern Mediterranean, the Americans have still found it a useful mobile support base, delivery platform and command centre – but it is being replaced in many navies by new types of vessels and aircraft with equal, if not greater, capability. It is perhaps no coincidence that the Soviet Navy, during its massive expansion programme of recent years, has not included conventional carriers in its equipment. With vessels like the Kiev – the nearest Soviet equivalent to the Thru'-Deck cruiser – and S/VTOL (short/vertical take-off and landing) aircraft such as the "Forger", there is no need. The techniques and equipment may have changed, but the importance of naval air support remains.

Maintenance
of air space

The final role to be examined – summed up by the phrase "the maintenance of air space" – is not easy to define. Perhaps the simplest way to understand it is in a peacetime context, when the air immediately above a country is internationally recognized as belonging to that country. Thus, if unauthorized aircraft fly through such air, they may be accused of violating the country's air space and run the risk of arrest or even destruction. In a war situation this concept obviously remains valid and is extended to include the air space above the country's armed forces, wherever they may be operating. As all air-power roles whether strategic or tactical, depend to a greater or lesser extent upon the ability of aircraft to move freely, the concept is clearly of paramount importance. Air warfare comes to depend upon the ability to defend or maintain air space while destroying that of the enemy. In other words, the aim is to gain air supremacy – a conquest of enemy air space which may be as effective in defeating him as a conquest of his territories on the ground.

Recognition of the possibilities along these lines undoubtedly came during the First World War. On the Western Front, for example, as soon as aircraft

began to be accepted as aggressive instruments of war, the maintenance of air space over the trench system became essential for secrecy in the planning of offensives and the protection of ground units from air attack. The evolution of the interceptor fighter, designed to carry out this task by destroying enemy reconnaissance and strike aircraft, has already been mentioned, together with the resultant "dog fights" between attacking and defending machines. As the war progressed, however, the Germans appear – yet again – to have been the first to develop the process to the extent of pursuing complete air supremacy, initially through the evolution of fighter "Circuses" (squadrons mobilized from place to place) which attempted to destroy enemy machines in the sky by totally swamping a particular area, and later by means of sustained attacks upon airfields and support services immediately behind the front line. Indeed, by 1917 the Royal Flying Corps was suffering so many losses, not only of aircraft but also of pilots, that German air supremacy was almost achieved. Fortunately for the Allies, a number of events, including the entry of America into the war and, perhaps no less importantly, the death of German

The air battles over the Western Front produced a few men more adept than most as pilots and tacticians; as they ran up a total of 'downed' enemy aircraft they joined that envied and short-lived group known as 'aces'. Two such, US Lt Frank Luke, Jnr left and Capt William Bishop, RFC below pose for pictures which would be treasured by an adoring public at home.

"Circus" leaders like Baron von Richthofen, combined to stop the rot, so that by 1918 it was the turn of the enemy the appreciate the necessity of maintaining air space as his armies came under unopposed air attack. By the end of the war the lesson had been learnt by both sides.

Meanwhile of course, with the Zeppelin and Gotha assaults on Britain, the maintenance of air space on the strategic level had become a matter of national security for one of the contending powers. This led to an increase in the anti-aircraft and fighter defences around the major English cities – which at least implied the possibility of counter-measures but seemed to suggest, through a conspicuous lack of success in 1917 and 1918, that air space was indefensible on a large scale.

This was perhaps an understandable point of view in the relatively unsophisticated days of the 1920s, but as the inter-war period progressed, technology once more swung firmly in favour of the defending side. On

the one hand interceptor-fighter design was greatly improved as a spin-off from the air races and air-speed record attempts of the 1930s. By the end of that decade the old biplanes which had experienced problems achieving the height and speed necessary for the destruction of incoming aircraft, had been largely replaced by sleek, fast, more heavily armed monoplanes like the Supermarine Spitfire and Messerschmitt Bf–109 which could hold their own against almost anything else that flew. At the same time, radar made its first appearance, giving to the defending country an instant ability to track attacking aircraft. This in turn gave time for the defending fighters to take up advantageous stations from which they could attack and destroy the hostile machines with the essential element of surprise on their side. These two improvements combined to undermine the belief that domestic air space was impossible to maintain in a war situation, as the Battle of Britain in 1940 effectively displayed.

After the fall of France in the summer of 1940 it seemed natural to expect the next stage of German conquest to be the islands of Britain, for if they remained a centre of opposition the entire western flank of Hitler's empire would be vulnerable. As a consequence, a German invasion of Britain appeared inevitable, particularly when the Royal Air Force reported a significant concentration of barges in the Channel ports of France and the Low Countries and German troops were known to be practising embarkation and disembarkation drills. But from the German side the invasion was not likely to stand much chance of success so long as air space above the invading forces was not secure, and as the majority of the Royal Air Force Fighter Command had survived the Dunkirk evacuation intact, the undefended barges were sure to come under air attack as they crossed the Channel. The Royal Air Force had therefore to be destroyed as an essential tactical preliminary to the entire operation: British air space, at least over the areas of the Channel and South coast, had to be effectively conquered.

This was clearly a task for the Luftwaffe, and the tactics employed appear to have centred initially, in August 1940, upon the idea of putting in bombing raids against targets which the Royal Air Force would be forced to defend, so bringing the Spitfires and Hurricanes into the open for piecemeal destruction by the German fighters. Victory would result, it was argued, simply because the Luftwaffe was numerically

P38J LIGHTNING

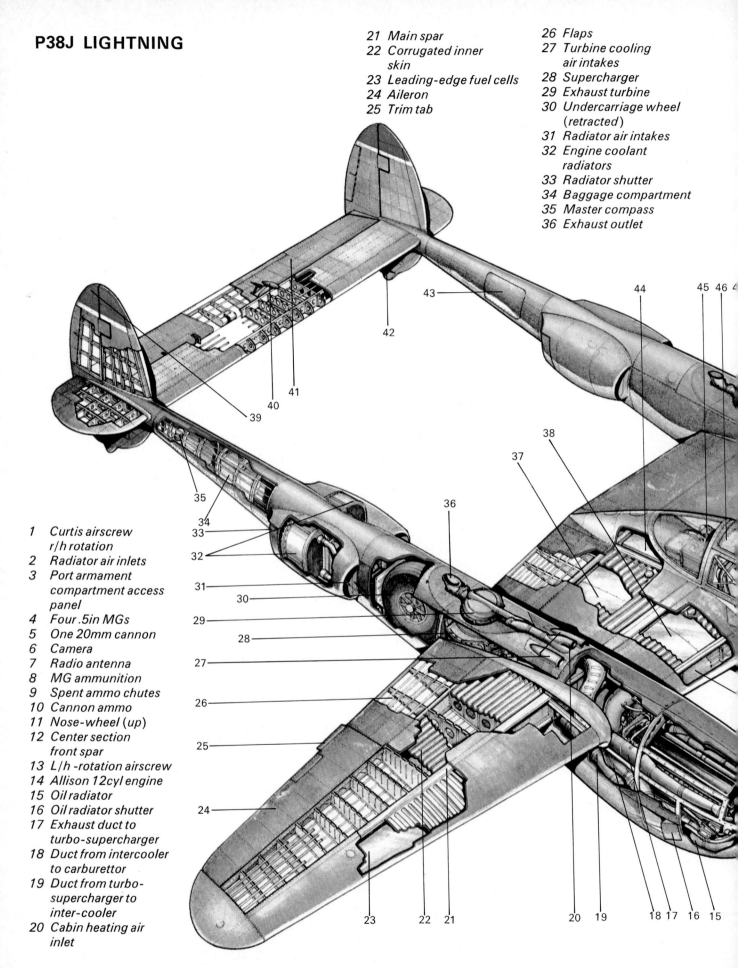

21 Main spar
22 Corrugated inner skin
23 Leading-edge fuel cells
24 Aileron
25 Trim tab

26 Flaps
27 Turbine cooling air intakes
28 Supercharger
29 Exhaust turbine
30 Undercarriage wheel (retracted)
31 Radiator air intakes
32 Engine coolant radiators
33 Radiator shutter
34 Baggage compartment
35 Master compass
36 Exhaust outlet

1 Curtis airscrew r/h rotation
2 Radiator air inlets
3 Port armament compartment access panel
4 Four .5in MGs
5 One 20mm cannon
6 Camera
7 Radio antenna
8 MG ammunition
9 Spent ammo chutes
10 Cannon ammo
11 Nose-wheel (up)
12 Center section front spar
13 L/h -rotation airscrew
14 Allison 12cyl engine
15 Oil radiator
16 Oil radiator shutter
17 Exhaust duct to turbo-supercharger
18 Duct from intercooler to carburettor
19 Duct from turbo-supercharger to inter-cooler
20 Cabin heating air inlet

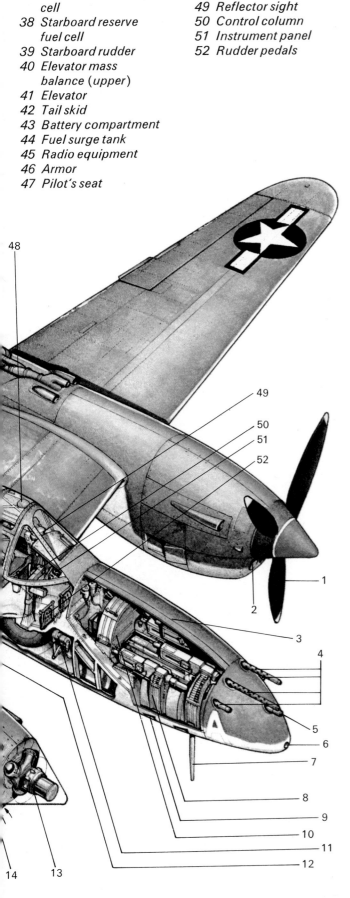

37 Starboard fuel
cell
38 Starboard reserve
fuel cell
39 Starboard rudder
40 Elevator mass
balance (upper)
41 Elevator
42 Tail skid
43 Battery compartment
44 Fuel surge tank
45 Radio equipment
46 Armor
47 Pilot's seat

48 Rear-view mirror
49 Reflector sight
50 Control column
51 Instrument panel
52 Rudder pedals

stronger and therefore capable of swamping the enemy – an interesting reversion to the "Circus" tactics of 1917. But things had changed dramatically since the First World War and, although the early raids against Channel convoys, port installations, radar stations and airfields did bring the Royal Air Force to battle, the Luftwaffe commanders had obviously underestimated the two defensive improvements of the inter-war years. The Spitfires and Hurricanes, despite their numerical inferiority, proved more than a match for the majority of Luftwaffe aircraft, forcing a complete withdrawal from the battle of the JU87 Stuka dive-bomber, which suffered crippling casualties in August alone. At the same time, although a number of radar stations on the south coast of England were attacked, the Germans do not seem to have regarded them as important, for enough were left intact for them to continue their essential early warning process, ordering the defending fighters into the sky in time to intercept the enemy raids and so achieve surprise. By mid-September 1940 the Luftwaffe was losing so many aircraft in British air space – a process which meant that any surviving crews automatically ended up as prisoners-of-war – that a change in tactics had to be made.

The ensuing alteration was of integral importance to the outcome of the Battle of Britain, for as the month of September drew to a close the Luftwaffe switched its aim away from the destruction of the Royal Air Force to a strategic bombing offensive against major British cities. As with all such offensives, it was hoped that the enemy's industrial base would be destroyed and the morale of the people undermined. In reality, all that it did was to give the RAF fighters and their support services a vital breathing space, during which their continuing hold over domestic air space was consolidated. The Luftwaffe attempted to by-pass the situation by bombing at night, but it soon became apparent that they had lost the battle. Their initial tactical aim, despite its feasibility, had not been achieved, forcing them into a long-term process of strategic bombing which did nothing to prepare the way for the invading forces. By late 1940 it was obvious that Hitler had lost all interest in Britain now that her defeat could not be obtained by a lightning stroke and, after his embroilment in Russia the following June, all thought of invasion entirely disappeared.

But if the pendulum of technological change had swung in favour of the British in 1940, it was clearly against them when they and their American allies tried

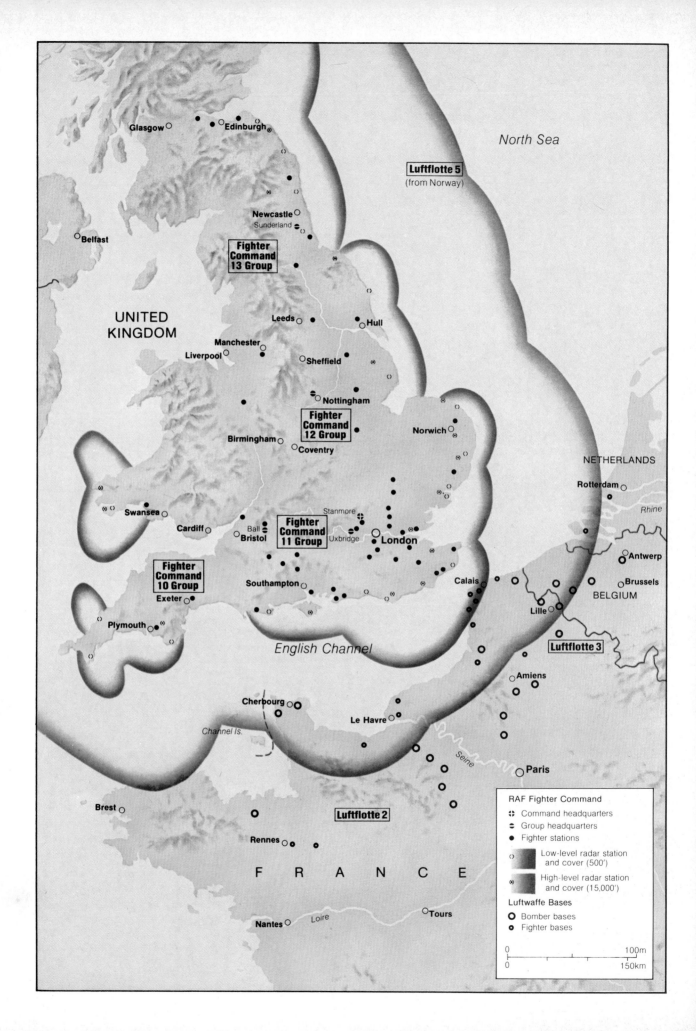

North Sea

Luftflotte 5
(from Norway)

Glasgow
Edinburgh

Belfast

Newcastle
Sunderland

**Fighter
Command
13 Group**

UNITED
KINGDOM

Leeds
Hull

Manchester
Liverpool
Sheffield

Nottingham

**Fighter
Command
12 Group**

Birmingham
Coventry

Norwich

NETHERLANDS

Rotterdam

Rhine

Swansea

Cardiff

Bristol
Ball

Stanmore

**Fighter
Command
11 Group**

Uxbridge
London

Antwerp

Brussels

BELGIUM

**Fighter
Command
10 Group**

Exeter

Southampton

Calais

Lille

Luftflotte 3

Plymouth

English Channel

Amiens

Cherbourg

Channel Is.

Le Havre

Seine

Paris

Brest

Luftflotte 2

Rennes

F   R   A   N   C   E

Nantes   *Loire*

Tours

RAF Fighter Command

⬦ Command headquarters

◗ Group headquarters

● Fighter stations

◖ Low-level radar station
and cover (500')

⊗ High-level radar station
and cover (15,000')

Luftwaffe Bases

◯ Bomber bases

◉ Fighter bases

0 ————————— 100m
0 ————————— 150km

74

A Messerschmitt 262 jet fighter caught in the camera guns of a diving Allied Mustang. The 262 was the last attempt to win control of German air space. Left: The Battle of Britain — without control of British air space the German navy and army would not have survived an assault on the British Isles. The margin of success and failure was very fine and the British 'victory' reflects the German decision to turn east and attack Russia.

to conquer German air space during the strategic bombing offensive upon the enemy homeland. We have already seen what happened when the Allied bombers tried to destroy German industrial targets: the British suffered losses up to 50 per cent of the committed force as early as 1939, while the Americans experienced the full effect of interceptor fighters and anti-aircraft defences during their raids on Schweinfurt in 1943. Indeed, by the latter date the Germans had developed their air-defence systems almost to perfection, using a combination of ground and air radar, fighter-control stations, good interceptor aircraft and effective anti-aircraft guns. In addition, their tactics were usually more than adequate: during the Schweinfurt raids, for example, radar and visual sightings guided the interceptors on to the B-17 "box" formations, whereupon the Americans were hit from every conceivable angle by almost anything that could fly. Messerschmitt 109 and 110 and Focke Wulf 190 fighters attacked the boxes from the front, sides and rear, and medium bombers even dropped fragmentation bombs from above. The American formations broke under the sheer weight of attack and the bombers were picked off one by one as the interceptors or anti-aircraft guns concentrated upon each in turn. Similarly, during the Royal Air Force night-time raids, radar was used to pinpoint the bomber stream and special night-fighters were guided into its midst, locating individual aircraft by means of air-radar and then attacking suddenly and invariably effectively. As late as March 1944, during a raid on Nuremberg, these tactics were working well enough for the Germans to destroy ninety-seven Lancasters and Halifaxes in one night. In such circumstances the defending power still seemed to hold much of the initiative.

The American decision to concentrate upon the total destruction of the Luftwaffe after late 1943 was clearly the turning point in Allied efforts to conquer German air space, although it is interesting to note that the basic tactics involved were very similar to those used by the Germans in 1917 and 1940. During the months when strategic bombing was possible in 1944, the Americans put in raids against targets the enemy was forced to defend, and when his interceptors arrived on the scene the P51 escort-fighters proved their worth by knocking them out of the sky. By the time of the D-Day invasion air space over the occupied countries of Western Europe was firmly in Allied hands, and by late 1944 the Luftwaffe had virtually ceased to exist. There can, of course, be little doubt that factors such as improved Allied offensive techniques, a growing lack of the vital materials needed to sustain the Luftwaffe, and the steady Allied advances on the ground all contributed to this destruction of German air superiority. However, the appearance and re-appearance of massed formations of Allied bombers and their escort-fighters day after day literally swamped the defensive capability of the Luftwaffe.

Events since 1945 reinforce this general conclusion, particularly in the context of the Arab-Israeli Wars. The Israelis, for instance, have come to depend for success upon the concept of mobile campaigns, not unlike the Second World War *blitzkrieg* idea, and for this they need to maintain complete air supremacy, at least immediately above and in front of their advancing ground forces. In the 1967 War this was achieved by means of the pre-emptive strike when, on the morning of June 5, the Israeli air force struck without warning at

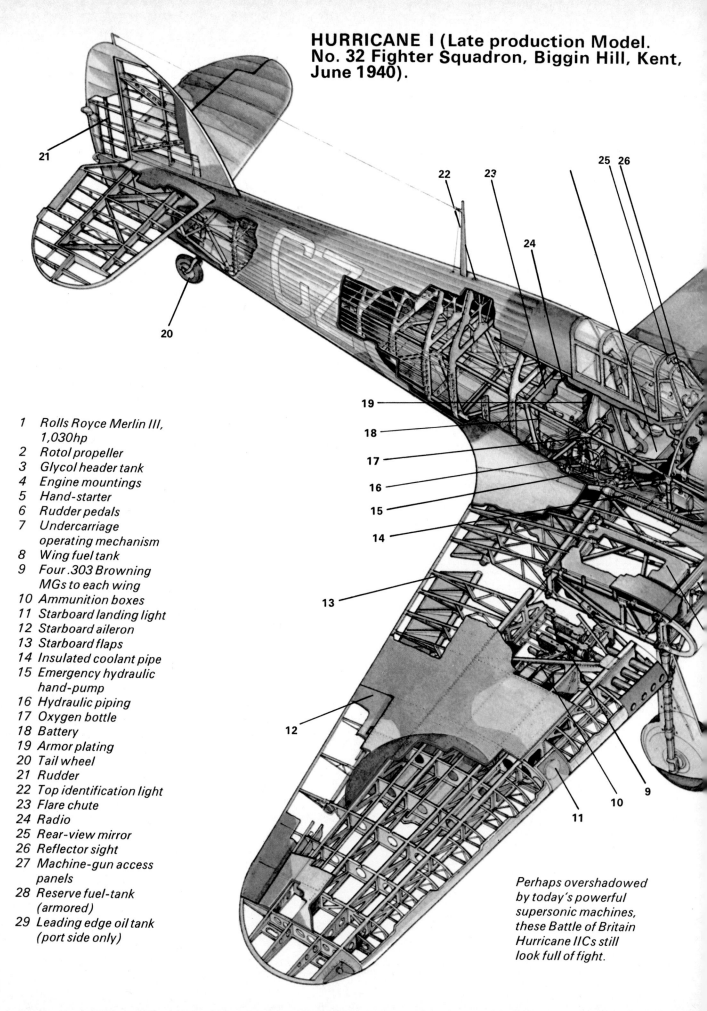

HURRICANE I (Late production Model. No. 32 Fighter Squadron, Biggin Hill, Kent, June 1940).

1 Rolls Royce Merlin III, 1,030hp
2 Rotol propeller
3 Glycol header tank
4 Engine mountings
5 Hand-starter
6 Rudder pedals
7 Undercarriage operating mechanism
8 Wing fuel tank
9 Four .303 Browning MGs to each wing
10 Ammunition boxes
11 Starboard landing light
12 Starboard aileron
13 Starboard flaps
14 Insulated coolant pipe
15 Emergency hydraulic hand-pump
16 Hydraulic piping
17 Oxygen bottle
18 Battery
19 Armor plating
20 Tail wheel
21 Rudder
22 Top identification light
23 Flare chute
24 Radio
25 Rear-view mirror
26 Reflector sight
27 Machine-gun access panels
28 Reserve fuel-tank (armored)
29 Leading edge oil tank (port side only)

Perhaps overshadowed by today's powerful supersonic machines, these Battle of Britain Hurricane IICs still look full of fight.

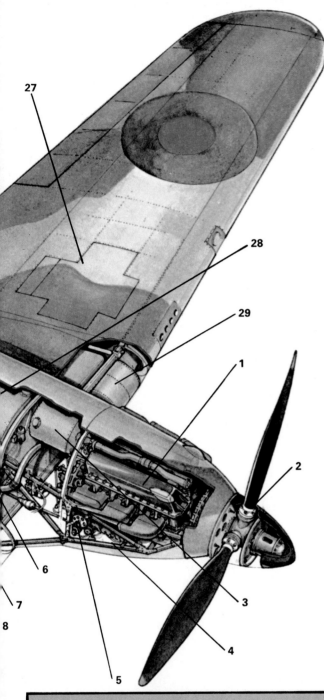

airfields in Egypt, Syria and Jordan. The Arab aircraft were dispersed in neat rows while their pilots and ground crews were at breakfast, and in less than three hours Egypt lost some 300 machines while the air forces of the other two states were entirely wiped out. This was the ultimate in the "swamping" technique of offensive air conquest, and led quite naturally to Israeli ground success as the armour and infantry units advanced into Sinai, Golan and Jerusalem unopposed by air attack. Arab air space had been conquered before the war had really begun.

Such brazen disregard for the niceties of war could hardly be repeated, however, and as soon as the Arab states recovered they began to improve their defensive positions for the future. With Russian aid, special hardened hangars were built to protect each of the replacement Mig fighters, and a completely new generation of anti-aircraft weapons was procured. In addition, when the next round of war broke out in October 1973, the Arabs made sure that they would escape another pre-emptive strike by attacking first, and when the Israeli Phantoms and Skyhawks tried to recover the initiative they encountered a solid wall of surface-to-air missiles and sophisticated anti-aircraft guns. The old SAM2s and 3s, which had proved little more than an irritant in 1967, had been replaced by mobile SAM6s and manportable SAM7s, while the radar-controlled ZSU-23-4s added a whole new dimension to effective air defence. Admittedly, the Israeli pilots did counter these measures to a certain extent, chiefly through Electronic Counter Measures (ECM) and a basic change in tactics which involved low-level attacks under the radar cover, but they lost valuable aircraft in the process and the idea of wide-ranging mobile ground offensives seemed extremely costly. The pendulum appeared still to be on the side of the defending power.

It is difficult to say to what extent this affects the situation today, particularly if we consider the Central Front in Europe should a war occur between NATO and the Warsaw Pact. So far as NATO, as the defending power, is concerned, technology appears to be acting in her favour, and with weapons systems such as Rapier, Blowpipe and Dragon available, Warsaw Pact air attacks upon the ground forces are likely to be opposed fairly effectively. But air warfare is a two-way business, and while the NATO forces are being protected in this manner, their air elements will be looking for opportunities to attack the enemy advance.

Right: An RAF Hawker Siddeley Harrier fires a salvo of air-to-ground rockets. The Harrier is also used by the US Marine Corps. Its vertical take-off capability allows it to be deployed close to the forward edge of the battle area.
Below: An American F86A Saber fires rockets at a ground target during the Korean War.

As the Warsaw Pact is equipped with many of the weapons used to effectively by the Arabs in 1973, and has of course improved them since that time, their air space too is going to be difficult to infiltrate. Air supremacy will have to be achieved by one side or the other if ground forces are to be effective, and the end result may be a return to the "swamping" technique, with either the pre-emptive strike or sheer numerical superiority tilting the balance. Since technology began to affect air warfare in the 1930s, these are the only measures which seem to have successfully countered the continuing defensive advantage in the maintenance of air space.

Conclusion

In order to sum up, a few general points only need to be made: firstly, it is apparent that the aircraft has never won a war alone using purely conventional weapons, despite the claims of the inter-war air theorists. The problems of mounting and executing a

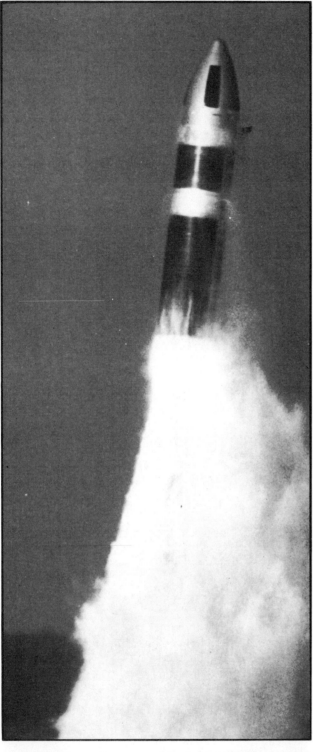

The weapons of deterrence: Below: A USAAF F-101 fighter fires a Genie air-to-air missile, the Genie has a range of up to six miles. Left: With a range of nearly 3000 miles, a Poseidon nuclear missile at the moment of launch from a submerged submarine.

successful bombing campaign on a strategic level are immense, and unless the weapons to be used are instantly devastating, the defending country will invariably be able to hold out for a substantial period of time. Nuclear weapons are powerful enough to provide this instant devastation, but their use would be self-defeating in an age of mutual assured destruction. For this reason, it is probable that a war involving their full-scale commitment will never occur. Such an argument, however, does call into serious question the strategic viability of air power, for although certain aspects of transport and reconnaissance could, in a select number of cases, be termed strategic in aim, they are nowhere near important enough to justify the ideas of Douhet or Mitchell. The first overall conclusions would therefore seem to be that the aircraft has never really discovered an effective place in the strategy of war.

But this should not be taken to mean that the impact of air power has been small, for as the second general point it is equally apparent that in the various tactical roles examined above, the aircraft has added a completely new and effective dimension to the face of modern battle. In the sphere of reconnaissance observation, it has enabled commanders to see "the other side of the hill" with unprecedented clarity; in that of tactical strike support interdiction the teeth of ground forces have been considerably sharpened; in the areas of transport, airborne landings, naval support and the maintenance of air space, increased flexibility, mobility, offensive and defensive powers have contributed to a string of remarkable success. Technology may cause the importance of these roles to fluctuate from time to time, but the tactical potential of air power remains. The pre-eminence of these tactical roles has been officially recognized, and a quote from Sir Andrew Humphrey, Chief of the British Defence Staff, appears to sum up the contribution of modern air power very well indeed. Writing in 1976, he says. "Control of the air in war involves not only the guaranteeing of free movement for our own troops and supplies, but also freedom to use the air space that matters to us for defence, offense, and reconnaissance while at the same time denying it to the enemy."

And to control the air, aircraft bring certain characteristics which are not shared by land or sea forces – the ability to carry weapons over long ranges at great speed, the ability to concentrate rapidly large forces over a distant point, the ability to switch targets and to surprise and deceive – in a word, flexibility.